Creative
Stress

Creative Stress

A Path for Evolving Souls
Living through Personal and
Planetary Upheaval

James
O'Dea

Book design and typography by Alden Bevington
Cover Image "Cosmic Eye" by Philomena O'Dea
Set in 11-point Adobe Caslon Pro by Piøneer Imprints
www.pioneerimprints.com
Pioneer Imprints
P.O. Box 600
Ross, CA 94957

Second Printing August, 2010

ISBN: 978-0-9818318-6-2

Library of congress cataloguing-in-publication data available upon request.

1 2 3 4 5 6 7 8 9 10—03 02 01

Dedicated to

*the creative energy of the
universe, its manifestation
in all evolving souls and
its expression in my sons
Luke, Brendan and Devin*

Contents

Acknowledgments

Great thanks to all who have guided me, and from whose wisdom and abundant creativity I have drawn deeply. Most especially, Jean Houston, Abdul Aziz Said, Michael Singer, Barbara Marx Hubbard, Sequoyah Trueblood, Kabir and Camille Helminski. I am deeply grateful to all those sacred activists and transformational agents who take the harshness and cruelty of the world and turn it into love, compassion and healing—most particularly colleagues in social healing work: Judith Thompson, Maureen Hetherington, Belvie Rooks and many more across the planet. Deep gratitude to Rich Meyer, Sandra Hobson, and Michael Singer for Fellowship support. Considerable thanks go to Mali Rowan for her steadfast multi-tasking and her courageous life, learning to face down fiercely negative stress and turning it to committed action.

Great appreciation to all my friends and colleagues in The Evolutionary Leaders group and to Deepak for providing such tremendous commitment to getting out there as a voice for personal and planetary transformation. To the Institute of Noetic Sciences, where after some years as its President, I remain a Fellow—thanks for giving me time to contemplate the marriage of science and spirituality and stimulating my imagination to envision the utter transformation of human consciousness.

And, finally, to Kathleen, my heartfelt acknowledgment that our wrenching storm was a part of Life's mysterious creativity!

Introduction

Stress is a primal force of nature. Without it life would have no impetus to push its way through. We would not mature and nothing would evolve. It meets us in the birth canal and comes for us at death. It is pure energy coming to tell us of approaching challenges, threats and dangers as well as breath-taking opportunities for courage, audacity and creativity. It is the same energy that tells us that action is needed, a response is required—and a choice has to be made.

Stress either opens us up or closes us off.

When it causes us to open, life does not get easier, it gets deeper, more creatively engaged and spiritually fulfilling. Overcoming our tendency to close is our most essential work, even when life throws boulders in our path or when it blinds us with unexpected tragedy.

When we close we turn our backs on Life as our teacher, and the lessons of unimaginable significance, that are offered to us for our growth and development. When we open, and then learn to open fully and completely, every stressful challenge we face becomes one more milestone in our heart's awakening and in the creative expression of our soul's desire to manifest its true purposes.

Stress has one thousand signature notes—from tinkling warning bell felt in the solar plexus, to alarms which race our pulse and bring us out in a sweat, all the way to full-scale sirens causing serious palpitations and major shock. Despite its ability to literally take over the normal functioning of our bodies and minds to say, *'Take note. Pay heed. Stop what you're doing!'* stress always invites you to respond in what ever way you choose. As difficult as it may be to regain control of the executive and decision-making functions of our brains and exercise conscious choice under severe stress—*that* is what is called for.

The more we build our self awareness and inhabit our own in-the-present consciousness, the more we will see that stress is not designed to take away free choice—in fact, more than anything else, it can serve to rivet your attention to the moment of choice. Of course it gets more alarmed if a response is lacking—*'Is anyone there? Is anyone home?'*—it seems to be saying, as it ratchets up your blood pressure and fuels booster rockets of adrenaline into your system.

Stress unattended to by an absent, immobilized, or confused conscious mind, turns from neutral to negative. Stress acknowledged, contextualized, and re-framed by the conscious mind's power of choice, will and intention turns from negative to positive— opening up a limitless field of creative   action.

You are standing on the edge of a terrifying sheer cliff with craggy rocks and churning waters below. As you prepare to jump your body panics in a sudden riot of stress signals warning you of extreme danger—yet you jump anyway. And you have the first thrill of the most exhilarating hang-gliding experience of your life!

While, for most of us, this is not an everyday experience, it reinforces a central concept in transforming negative into creative stress: your conscious mind is where decisions must get made. When I say conscious mind, I mean the full array of your heart-mind-spirit intelligence. Allowing your body's stress mechanisms to signal to you, without direct response from the conscious mind, is only to invite them to continue to escalate their signaling and eventually to stir up trouble if unattended.

In the case of the hang-glider, once she leaves solid ground and takes to the air—it is not as if stress signals are not continuing to pour in—there is a physical stress which takes the form of, *'Hold tight for dear life.'* There is cognitive stress. *'You are defying gravity, you need to sensitively adjust to air currents to make a safe landing'*—and so on. But because there is conscious choice to fully experience all these sensations and gain mastery over fear, these primary stress mechanisms are now the source of single-minded purpose and a sense of achievement and sheer delight.

Stress reveals the fault lines of our psyche and the bedrock of our character like no power on earth. It traces the contours of our phobias and inhibitions, and it also marks with precision, the places where we go beyond our fears to create new experience and to live to our highest potential. It is often the spur to deep self-discovery.

Stress can snag us, pull us up short and cause us to pause—and if we are not careful the pause is protracted into a longer stall, and can even precipitate a sickening downward spiral. It is also—without doubt—the catalyst for movement, for great achievement and profound transformation. Stress cracks the shell and offers us the kernel! It forces us to go beyond appearances, *'Show me your true face. Let me see what you are really made of,'* it seems to be saying. It asks us to reveal our essence, the way a diamond must be washed and polished for its beauty to be made visible.

We know that stress can be self-imprisoning: cutting us off from manifesting our most dynamic qualities—somehow muffling and submerging our unique charisma in a haze of false accommodations and compromises. It has the power to dig us into a gloomy underworld of regret, disappointment, shame, unresolved anger and self-pity—and finally, into an even gloomier dungeon of perpetual fear, rage and victimization—where we throw away the key to health and peace of mind.

For some, stress is the path to ill health and ruin, for others it is a catalyst for transformation; some remain trapped in negative stress, others find their freedom through creative stress.

While negative stress can spin between suppression and explosion, creative stress engages directly and articulates boldly.

While negative stress swings between passivity and volatility, creative stress modulates the tension and channels energy into fruitful action.

While negative stress victimizes others or perpetuates a state of victimhood, creative stress takes responsibility, avoids scapegoating and seeks to heal and to restore strength.

While negative stress is punitive and demands vindication, creative stress seeks to resolve conflict, and cultivate qualities of forgiveness and compassion.

While negative stress feeds off inadequacy, or an inflated sense of worth, creative stress transcends the ego's false reality and dives into soul power.

Since there is a huge body of research on negative stress, we will consider that territory well-covered and only refer to it where necessary, this book is about *transforming* negative stress, not *dwelling* upon its detrimental effects.

However, we will not flinch from examining the role of pain, suffering and grievous wounding in catalyzing the highest human creativity.

Creative Stress is not a book about *stress-light* or how to live a 'low-stress' life. Nor is it about how to relax. It is about *understanding how to engage stress in ways that lift us upward towards our highest creative capacities*. It is about the psychological and spiritual development that emerges out of an authentic effort to face our fears, meet our demons and engage the truth of who we are at the core—so that we tap well-springs of creative insight and energy, and live the gift of who we are in a dynamic and uncompromised way.

Creative Stress sees stress as a phenomenal force in nature—one that will inevitably enter our lives in the most personal and intimate ways as we struggle not only to survive, but to evolve and to realize our full personal and collective potential. Stress presents itself as a challenge to the status quo, it says, *'Time to move on. Time to grow some more. Time to move beyond limited self-interest.'* As the very engine of evolutionary change, it plays its own key role in the work of humanizing societies and in moving us towards a more sustainable and just global order.

We live at a time of acute planetary stress—for humans, and for all species—*Creative Stress* is an invitation to stop digging our own grave and to embrace the challenges we face with new vitality, greater wisdom and spiritual maturity. From the personal to the global, our most defining choices will be how we transform corrosively negative stress into a healthy, sustainable, peaceful and creatively charged future. To achieve these lofty goals we must be prepared to grow and grow and grow—as we learn to transform negative stress into creative energy, we are *initiated step-by-step* in the journey towards our very highest potential. The journey takes many different forms, but whatever form it takes, as the mystics remind us, "*the heart must face its tests.*" Only then, can we discover who we really are and what extraordinary things we are capable of achieving.

1

Exploring the Basics
of Creative Stress

You have a router for every energy that comes into your body: it literally switches the energy in one direction or another. Just as you have arteries for your blood, you have neural highways that convey your responses to whatever energy is coming at you. You are swarming with internal traffic cops who wave you on, bring you to a halt or tell you to take a detour…and they switch and re-direct in nano seconds; they are faster than our fastest computers. This routing system is full of instant commands: '*Proceed! Welcome! Back-off! Avoid! Ignore! Ask for more! Blush! Run for your life! Reject! Embrace!*'

A good number of these responses come with your basic mind-body equipment—and encode millions of years of evolutionary learning and represent adaptation to changing environments over vast stretches of time. Because of

1

this shared and inherited field of learning you can react and respond at almost instantaneous speed to changing conditions around you. This gives you a platform for communication—you don't have to invent things from scratch. The template for our instinctual selves is influenced by social and cultural conditioning, family patterns and personal choice. In addition we have conscious awareness. Consciousness, with its powers of deep attention and creative intention, is a pivotal driver of our personal and collective experience.

If we left our consciousness at the level of instinctual response we could not evolve as a species: the human story is one in which we collectively awaken to greater powers and capacities within this mysteriously expansive field of consciousness. Consciousness has the capacity to override our instincts; when we feel our blood boiling up in anger in response to some perceived threat or danger, our mind can sort through the situation and make skillful and creative choices based on moral and philosophical insights and our own originality, which diffuse *the fight response* with experiments in *dialogue and negotiation* or other techniques of compassionate engagement. This can happen as effortlessly and as fluently as any other more instinctive or triggered response, but it requires the cultivation of awareness and a whole new relationship to stress.

Learning to make skillful and creative choices is at the heart of this concept of creative stress. In order to become really skillful, the first thing you will have to study is that routing system and how it often seems to be responding *mechanically*—as if its instructions were *preset*, or for some, the feeling that they may be even preordained.

Let us examine what is going to inhibit a creative and insightful response to any situation likely to zap you with negative stress with all of its attendant discomfort, anxiety, fear, frustration or deeper distress.

The three responses which will prevent you from transforming negative stress are:

- *the non-response*
- *the inauthentic response*
- *the make matters worse response*

In each case your routing system for any incoming energy which has the potential to leave you feeling negatively stressed has an automatic default—ignore, send decoy or attack.

The Non-Response: Ignore

Your body has a FedEx department. It works very hard to have an efficient urgent delivery service. Just contemplate the vast network of cellular, neural, electrical and biochemical processes it mobilizes to deliver you signals faster than the speed of light; all in service to your welfare, safety and well-being. More than a little *appreciation* is deserved for its miraculous design—no piece of technology humans have invented comes anyway close to the body's nano-second responsiveness, adaptability and creativity.

So naturally, something is wrong if it is ignored—how after all, is it going to genetically encode your responses if you pretend you do not hear the body signaling to you? You can be sure that the body will not understand the non-response to its tapping at the door of your conscious mind. *It will knock louder and louder.* You hardly need me to tell you that stress ignored builds over time. Although you might think it can be silenced, or its very existence denied, your body will eventually send system-wide alerts to your organs until you eventually have to stop and listen to it. Sadly, by then, you may be chronically adverse to dealing with, and responding to, the body's naturally communicative stress signals. In such cases people can move from thriving to merely surviving.

'*I am not going to let this upset me*,' is an understandable response to situations that provoke negative feelings in you, but if your default strategy is to deny the reality that you are being aroused for a reason, then you are storing up a problem rather than engaging a solution. The non-response stockpiles raw, unprocessed energy which is left to stagnate and become increasingly toxic.

At a planetary and species-wide level we are discovering how much we have collectively shut off our responses to the deep stress signals in Nature. We may now be slowly waking up to the screams of distress in the natural world as we witness the loss of species across the planet and the nightmare scenarios of global warming and climate imbalance. The story of our pervasive damage to our Earth habitat is a story about our inability to attend to stress and our lack of understanding about how to meet our challenges, even great ones, energetically, decisively and creatively. But, slowly it seems, we are being roused from an artificial cocoon of excessive materialism and deep distraction by the scale and severity of evolutionary stresses which can no longer be ignored. For to ignore them will sound our collective death knell. To attend to them, however late in the day, will engage us in transforming current conditions in ways that may usher in a new era of planetary civilization. Even late in the day, *when the call is answered*, healing begins.

The Inauthentic Response: Send a Decoy

So here we are back at the router again: some high velocity energy is coming towards you and it is clear that there is no way to ignore it, and so the energy is deflected and channeled into a fiction or a distraction—something that pretends to deal with energy that is felt to be too hot to handle directly. Your body knows immediately if you are not engaging with the energy directly, or truthfully. Basically, what you're saying to this energy is, '*I can't handle you. But I'm in a situation where it is too embarrassing to ignore you. So I am going to have to make a pretense.*'

What you do in those situations has a lot to do with personality and patterns that have developed since childhood in the way you deal with stress. It's worth spending a little time to become aware of your default mode when you're being *less than authentic.*

Examples of inauthentic responses to stress:

You fake being nice when you want to get out from under the heels of a difficult person or difficult situation.

You create a distraction, changing the subject or doing something which will draw attention away from your need to give an honest response.

You divert attention with a negative decoy; transferring blame or complaint elsewhere.

You use seduction and insincere compliments to gloss over the thing that needs to be addressed.

You lie: from tiny little white lies to ones which really matter.

And all this happens in the twinkling of an eye as stressful energy gets rerouted and not dealt with. I suggest you might want to do your own little research study and note how often your own communication, or that of others around you, is inauthentic.

For your own emotional, psychological and spiritual growth, it is essential to learn how to be completely authentic. Trying to make life easier, sweeter and more pleasing for everyone around you is a sure fire way to build up reservoirs of negative stress—and that energy will one day get released in ways that generally won't be pretty or nice. Your personal growth really begins when you see, however difficult it is to be your authentic self, that this approach transforms negative stress.

We live in an age when we are waking up to the fact that we have buried ourselves in materialistic distractions rather than facing with real integrity the challenges that face humanity. From outrageous political spin and pompous media punditry to multiple forms of techno-distraction, we will not go down in history as an era of grounded truthfulness or authentic communication. What we are learning from this level of distraction is that *our stress has only been building* the more inauthentic things get.

The Make Matters Worse Response: Attack

This one is easy isn't it—for every energy which comes at you that you can't handle you send it back at twice the strength in order to keep it away. It says that the only way to survive is to be armed and dangerous and to make sure that you are on top. Ironically this approach, in being completely stress avoidant, creates the most short- and long-term negative stress. The attack mode prevents creativity; its purpose is to subordinate and control others. It says, *'I will be defended at all costs. I don't have to look inside for answers because the solutions are obvious to me.'*

There is not too much we need to say about how destructive this approach is. Self-defense does not need to take the form of attacking others. War is often a desperate resort of incompetence—when, in reality, every skillful means must be employed to avoid it. We also live in an era in which some of the heaviest investment in our future is in building more weapons of war. It is imperative that we invest twice as much in peace building, societal healing, and dialogic and negotiation skills. At the personal and collective level, the only path to inner and outer peace will emerge from creatively reaching out to solve our problems—that work requires significantly more sophisticated emotional, psychological and spiritual development than the starting place which says, *'Let's put our greatest resources into preparations to destroy each other.'*

So what is meant by the term *Creative Stress?*

We have created a false polarity between stress and relaxation—as if one is good for us and the other is bad. The shelves of bookstores are filled with stress reduction techniques and the medical profession and pharmaceutical industry have a cornucopia of stress reducing, calming, sleep-inducing drugs to help you de-stress.

What we need to be clearer about is exactly how we go about transforming negative stress into positive creative energy, not just finding ways to tamp it down until we no longer feel it. The greatest relaxation can come from resolving the unresolved, and from facing the cause of nagging stress. Yet even when we engage stress we can find ourselves initially challenged by more stress. But it's a different kind of stress…as paradoxical as it sounds, purposeful, self-initiated stress can be a perfect antidote to the stress that comes from that undercurrent of gnawing, unresolved, and paralyzing energy.

The science of stress tells us clearly that the stress mechanism cannot be ignored without significant damage to health. Stress must either be switched off or it must be engaged in ways which literally harness its energies in forms of creative action. When it is engaged, *even when stressful conditions persist,* transformation occurs. Its negative potential—however exacting, painful or exhausting—gets transformed as part of our affirmation of Life and our commitment to growth.

All heroic and courageous action relies on our creative engagement with stress.

All forms of artistic mastery rely on our creative engagement with stress.

Scientific progress emerges out of our creative engagement with stress.

Leadership is quintessentially the art of creatively engaging stress.

Happiness is not achieved without creative engagement with stress.

Healthy relationships cannot be sustained without creative engagement with stress.

Societies cannot evolve without creative engagement with stress.

So, creative stress is the energy and potential of your deeper, wiser self drawing you upward towards fulfillment, authenticity, and integrity. This energy does not seek either the easiest or the hardest way, it looks for *the most accurate way* to allow you to express the qualities of your higher being. It reminds you that each stress is an initiation that can open you up to the truth of who it is you are—that is where peace is to be found. If you find yourself de-stressing at the spa or by a beach sipping your favorite drink—and you find that you are really only superficially relaxed and still frustrated or bored, or your mind is scurrying around like a chicken without its head; if you're honest, you'll admit that the antidote to negative stress is not relaxation but an inner peace that comes from being aligned with your core being.

As you learn to transform negative stress as a path to your higher self, you become more subtle, more alive in your core passion, more conscious of others' potential and more compassionate about how we suffer in the process of self-discovery. Isn't that worth experiencing rather than looking for the next escape chute? Or living with that perpetual whine, '*I am so stressed,*' as if you were permanently a victim of circumstances beyond your control.

The Three Levels of Creative Stress

Level One: The Direct Encounter

Stress can pounce on you with alacrity and with various degrees of severity: without warning, someone you love gets ill or dies tragically—you lose your job—a lawsuit or divorce papers land at your door—your kid is arrested, in possession of drugs—you do not have enough money to pay the bills—you have been speeding and the police officer appears out of nowhere with flashing lights—you discover your boyfriend has been cheating. Almost no day passes without an encounter with one form of stress or another, some of it minor, some of it deeply challenging. These kind of stress-producing situations, as we have noted, can trigger a variety of responses or even a suppression response.

While there are no neat and tidy right ways to respond, what we want to aim for is something beyond a brush off, a blame response—but rather a direct encounter with stress. In this approach we are prepared to face *the reason this incident or situation is stressful for us.* If we do not have this direct encounter with stress, it will be difficult to transform its energy and charge in a positive direction.

The direct encounter does not seek to deflect or get rid of stress as soon as possible, nor is it immobilized by stress. In some ways you could say stress is approached like a stern or fastidious teacher who wants to make sure we fully absorb the depth of the lesson. In this approach we let the discomfort stay long enough to learn from it. And maybe even find ourselves radically surprised by what at first appeared to be grueling! The direct encounter with stress is a strategy that can lead to more positive outcomes because we are willing to engage, or even wrestle with, what is triggering us. When we have a direct encounter with stress we begin to grapple with what it *means* that we are upset, worried, angry or wounded. We start using the deeper stuff of our own awareness to be just a little more self-reflective. The direct encounter is an approach to a wide range of possible responses to stress which selects growth, learning, improvement, and insight.

It is the beginning of the cultivation of wisdom.

The direct encounter with stress is a strategy built upon an attempt to live with integrity—we're willing to forgo cheap explanations or engage in blame. *We face the music.* If we allow ourselves to experience the full impact of our fears—fear of loss, separation, blame, insufficiency, inadequacy, disappointment—we can dissolve their negative power and create new meaning in our lives where we would not have thought it possible. But that power to dissolve negative energy is not gained without the courage to grasp the nettle or look in the mirror…it is a stance that allows the bitter to be fully tasted as bitter, and not be sugar-coated.

The direct encounter with stress opens us to deeper questions:

'How did this happen? What does this mean? What is the situation asking of me? How can I behave differently? What insights can I gain? What can I learn from this? What am I called to be?'

In the direct encounter we can find ourselves wrestling with difficult truths. It's as if the stress we are experiencing is prodding us to go further—to get to the bottom of bigger issues. The stress is sustained *long enough* to make us so uncomfortable that we want to enact change. We discover that change does not necessarily come easily, so we find -ourselves pulled back and forth. *'Should I leave, shouldn't I leave? Shall I tell them, shall I keep it secret? 'Will they be able to bear it if I tell the whole truth?'* The direct encounter with stress keeps us agonizing for a while, *grappling with meaning* itself!

This is precisely the zone in which we can feel the pull to act not just out of ego-survival but from a higher place. Because we are struggling and even uncertain about which path to choose, we find that options that were hidden or obstructed, can now come into play. We realize we have an opportunity to unburden our soul in a way that is new and even refreshing. New insights are available to us. We see where we have been unconsciously blocking the very expression of our own unique creativity. We find that we have the resources to summon up the courage which we hadn't known was there. We see that we are freer than we thought to live our convictions. In the direct encounter, because things are neither easy nor automatic, *something new can emerge from the churning* that we experience as we wrestle with finding the best way forward.

There is no doubt that facing the cause of our stress can leave us feeling skewered—we know that the way ahead may not be easy, but current conditions are not easy either. These can be times when it seems that the support we need is absent—it is almost as if the universe has conspired to make sure that we go deep into ourselves and find a way forward so that we can evolve to a higher ethical place; or grow to be more loving and compassionate; or simply discover that we have the inner strength and resources needed to face life's unavoidable challenges.

When we transform negative stress into positive and creative energy to deal with whatever difficulties come our way, we can sincerely look back at some of the worst experiences in our lives and *acknowledge* that they were instrumental in moving us to a more honest, integrated or healthier place in our lives. And we will know that our growing pains were worth it, for they were nothing less than initiations in the mystery of our own becoming.

Level Two: The Handshake

Denial of stress, or cute pseudo-techniques to dismiss it quickly, only delay our encounter with growing stress, and while that is happening, it is gaining negative momentum. Then, when the dikes finally burst, we may find our health is significantly debilitated from accumulated stress! Once we face it, we begin to open the path to positive changes in our lives. This direct encounter, as we have just noted, is where we wrestle with confusion, balk for a while at the price of growth, and even meet our rowdier demons. But if we commit to an honest effort in addressing the real root causes of our stress, we *instigate changes in our lives* and develop a replenished will and resolve even when stressful conditions persist beyond our control.

Honing our capacity for honest encounters with whatever reality puts in our path, waters and nourishes our *conscience*. Conscience is not an insert into our psyche or physiognomy that simply goes on automatic pilot—as if we could say, *'Don't worry about it, my conscience will sort it out for me.'* It is no coincidence that we talk about *examining* our conscience—because it is tested, and it is constantly under the scrutiny of our higher self. The more it is tested, the more our conscience seems to develop its discerning muscle. It becomes more acute, more sensitive, more alive when it is engaged. Like consciousness, it grows and expands the more aware of it we are. Out of the cauldron of wrestling with our conscience and in response to stressful nudging and prompting, we gain a fresh ability and greater skillfulness in dealing with Life's challenges. Now we are ready for the next stage of our growth: when stress comes our way, rather than ignoring it, or even grimly facing it, we greet it and shake its hand!

Sound unreal? It is, on the contrary, a great sign of mental and emotional health, and growing psychological and spiritual maturity, when we are able to *greet* our difficulties and challenges.

A handshake can be a symbolic act of respect and courtesy and it can signify everything from non-hostility to warmth and friendship. Nonetheless, despite this large variance in significations, a handshake, if it is genuine, reflects openness. In relationship to stress it is a posture which says,

'I recognize you. I have learned that you have the ability to teach me. I want to grow. I am even energized by the pain or difficulty that you present because I know that it can help free me to become a bigger, better, and wiser human being.'

Now let me assure you that this is not playschool Pollyanna: you are now prepared to have a full and direct encounter with anxiety, worry, fear, painful loss, separation—whatever it takes—*but you do so in the knowledge that you are going to benefit.* This must mean that you have begun to develop some confidence in your capacity to live deeply, some skillfulness at mobilizing the will to face truth at any cost, and to create a more *meaningful* life for yourself in the process. It is not that you go looking for difficulty and challenge, but that you have learned that stress can never take away some deeper composure in your being. Even if stress comes at you like an adversary, you treat it like a noble adversary.

Your life is anchored in a deep inner knowing that carries you through all your challenges and difficulties. This is faith. By that, I do not mean church and religion. I mean the faith which has no intermediary between you and Life—that raw and elemental energy which is capable of enduring the greatest testing. *When, at last, you are able to shake hands with your difficulties you are ready to represent the power of your soul: your expanded inner nature.*

This is the beginning of a truly spirit-anchored life—in the sense that your inner life is not so externally dependent. The scales have tipped away from an imbalance in which every external phenomena was able to cause internal displacement—the place where we are knocked off kilter by the things that come at us in the world. In the handshake, the *center of gravity has shifted inside of our being* so that we feel a greater inner aliveness.

This is where self-knowledge begins.

This should not be confused with the state of bravado that declares, *'Throw all you have at me, Life, I can take it. Bring it on baby!'* Courting disaster is a sign of immaturity and reflects the absence of inner balance. It is actually saying, *'I really don't know who I am but at least I can show others how good I am at slaying dragons—or making millions—or wooing the masses!'* No, the handshake is more subtle than that.

Visualize one of those deep, graceful, oriental bows where even opponents show a certain humility towards each other—imagine yourself meeting an aggressive force coming towards you and that you are able to employ the precise amount of energy needed to disable it—like an aikido master. See yourself as tragic news is brought to you, knowing that more is going to be called from you than ever before in your life, but that you have deep reservoirs of strength to draw upon, and a greater measure of insight and wisdom to respond with.

When you have begun to master the handshake with stress you come into your own power as a creative agent in the world: remember stress never goes away, but it either creates obstacles or it creates flow, wrecks lives or provokes our higher powers. Knowing this, why wouldn't you greet it?

Level Three: The Embrace

If the Direct Encounter with stress may, at first, be little more than non-avoidance, it heralds a first acceptance that problems arise when you do not deal with stress. It is your way of saying to your soul and your psyche, *'I want to live a real life—an honest and ethical life and if that means I have to face these difficulties—so be it.'* You are not looking for the *easy* way out, you are looking for the *right* way forward.

This means you are even ready to wrestle with questions, confusion, agonizing uncertainty, rather than jump into a quick solution that you know will, in the long run, be a distraction or a band-aid. This approach brings a deepening quality and greater maturity to our lives—we now move more seamlessly into a kind of willing apprenticeship with Life's more difficult lessons. At this point the handshake with stress as a teacher, an initiator, is, as we have noted, accompanied with greater humility and understanding. We are able to appreciate that *the shocks and strains* of living are more than wretched and unfortunate experiences, they help us grow. They even illuminate our better natures or the parts of ourselves we still have to work on. We move from being a kind of honest broker in the direct encounter approach, to being a little wiser and more compassionate as we open ourselves to whatever is placed before us. Others can often see in us a deeper spirit and a wiser nature when we have reached this stage.

We all can think back on teachers or parents or grandparents who were able to share with us that loving demeanor of a person who, having faced hardships, multiple stresses and challenges, were also able to hold a natural dignity and a quiet reverence for life's unpredictable highs and lows. They remind us that the Handshake represents a way of reaching out to Life and offering to give it our best. In this phase of our development we do not recoil from negative stress, nor even spend much time wrestling with it, we engage it with a kind of awe which knows that our hardest lessons are our finest teachers. There is less *melodrama* and more soulful problem-solving and quiet discernment—when things fall apart we see that new opportunities can emerge in a natural and unforced way.

So you are now moving into a phase of your development where you see you are not really talking about managing stress so much as transforming it. You understand that what is required is that you be more honest with yourself, more compassionate to others, a better listener, and less prone to solving other's problems before you deal more credibly with your own issues. As we learn how to creatively engage with stress, we experience the delight of discovering inner resources we did not know we had. We sense the mystery of capacity, of being, of growing, of being filled with gratitude despite wounding, betrayal and, perhaps, tragic loss.

If you keep growing, at this point you will be ready to *embrace* stress because you have gained wisdom and spiritual insight into the meaning of your life.

You have gained a deeper sense of the enduring aspect of spirit and experienced its indomitable nature.

You will now experience what it is to be drawn towards wholeness rather than frenzy and fragmentation. You will know more fully the difference between just coping and feeling the presence of a more sustained daily nourishment of healing. You will experience healing radiating out from the center of a nourished heart. You will discover that people are *drawn* to your energy rather than *repelled* by it. You will also see that your ability to nourish yourself provides you with a greater abundance of energy to nourish others.

In the Embrace we are talking about a state of being that lives in communion with life itself. It is not caught in that endless game of *mental ping-pong* where the mind is constantly exploring what will make it happier—it has found its way to the root of joy.

Joy comes when there is unconditional acceptance, genuine forgiveness, and appreciation of experience, both good and bad, bitter and sweet. It is a place where we move from instances of passionate faith and conviction to abiding faith and effortless resolve to live in deeper harmony with all that comes our way. This is where our moral principles become fully integrated into capacities of empathy, love and compassion. This is also where our service towards others does not require ego-gratification and where it is an expression of higher vision. Now even when we are betrayed, we cannot be deflected from our commitment to carry on living in service to our own soul's calling. In this stage of mastery, when the world calls, it is not our frazzled psyche which responds, but our highest self.

This is a place of deep surrender to an integral reality—one in which there is no narrow artificial distinction or separation between our inner life and its outward manifestation in the world. It is a place of high spiritual attainment where negative energy is transformed: there is no place of self-deception where lower energy can attach itself; no place of deflection where the energy is bounced into holding tanks that fill up in concentrated toxicity; no place of grasping or attachment that specifically privileges certain areas of one's life as off bounds to stress. This is a place of intense humility, quiet discernment, and seasoned wisdom.

In the Handshake there is still measurable reserve, and the desire to negotiate the best solutions to keep one's ego fed and happy—in the Embrace, the ego has been disarmed and an inner transformation of such magnitude has been experienced that all armoring and defensiveness has dissolved into an intensified state of being which is ever-present to whatever arises. When we have developed deep presence, we are no longer trying to make things happen in the way we need them to happen—or when we were less mature, the way we *desperately* needed them to happen.

This does not mean that we fall into an '*anything goes*' approach or that we do not care about outcomes. When we are fully present and not trying to fix outcomes to match our personal and specific needs—we literally stop always identifying from a narrow personal space, which can find itself constantly trying to hold down the fort against a perceived enemy, and instead begin to identify trans-personally. We identify with the whole situation, *we identify with self—and—others simultaneously*. In this state we can begin to perceive much more clearly the source of accumulated energy blockages, and our only desire is now to address the root causes of distress, hurt, pain, and suffering caused by trapped and spinning negative stress.

Progress far enough into this state and we become truly free. We become doctors of the soul. We are able to be aikido masters of stress and servants of the highest good. Ultimately we will have moved all the way from deeply dependent consumers feeding off of all kinds of need, recognition attachment, fear avoidance, me first, to powerful universal beings who literally take this raw, crude, primal energy of the world and transform it into grace, love, compassion, boundless generosity, service and servant leadership.

Visualize moments when you were caught in the jaws of a hissy, toxic anger or resentment. You were just seething in the cauldron of some private hurt and along came a force, or presence, that began to dissolve that poisonous and *self-created* stress. Visualize the presence of the mother whose love dissolves your temper tantrum, the lover whose arms call you back into a state of intimate union, the dear friend whose steadfast journey by your side allows you to see that you have the power to release your resentments, and see that wise one you thought had abandoned you, who was really waiting to catch you in the deepest of all embraces when you fell.

All of these are faces of the great embrace that is the creative heart of a universe which conspires to draw you to your highest self. It lures you out of your lesser self, and lets you shed all that is not of your true essence so that you can be a full expression of creative spirit in action. The great sages and mystics who reach the complete realization of this state know that once you embrace all, you yourself are held in an embrace that is absolute acceptance and unimpeded grace.

Now visualize humanity growing through all its colossal and ravaging stress — through era after era of testing and challenge—in its collective movement towards these higher expressions of conscience and deeper expressions of psychological and spiritual growth. See the vistas that lie before us where our mighty challenges are transformed through love, wisdom, understanding and consciousness. See the emergence of a new humanity that restores its deeply wounded relationship with all of Nature's forms. See a service to the whole which transforms exploitation, vengeance, and punishment into new expressions of healing, justice and reconciliation. See the marriage of economy and ecology, of science and spirituality, and the reemergence of healthy and sustainable communities across the planet. And see in every stress that was transformed into creative response a benchmark in the history of life on this planet.

Then, one day, our descendents will turn and look at all those benchmarks of our collective spiritual emergence as a species and they will see what a price was paid, how much suffering and testing was endured, but they will also see that the greatest of all turning points was when we discovered how to ride energy so that it did not topple and drown us. They will point to the day when we learned to skillfully use energy to guide us and to lift us higher and higher into an evolving consciousness and towards the creative expression of inspired mind synchronized at last with our highest intentions for planetary peace and collective well-being.

.level one.

the direct encounter

2

Learning to Face Your Teacher

The direct encounter with stress is nothing less than a direct encounter with truth. It is about the holder of truth and the maker of meaning in your life, *which is you*. You are more than your impulses, your biological responses, your culturally conditioned and other inherited frameworks of meaning. You are a conscious being who has to learn how to negotiate these multiple influences on your thoughts, desires, and actions. There is a *you* there to encounter reality—a core identity that, at its deepest level, or its source point, we call your soul. As triggered and reactive as we might get, as confused, trapped or pushed into a corner as we can at times end up, we are not the things that happen to us. We are actually always at the center of what is happening around us. *Locate that center* and you will not only begin to ensure that you change your relationship to stress but you will begin to feel the presence of your own higher being.

Let's keep the spotlight on that elusive *you* for a moment longer. That you, however dazzled, spun, or buffeted by dramatic events or circumstances in your life, is a living awareness. It is your essence, not a peripheral thing, like a light switch that can get turned on or off. It is the sun in the sky of your being. Even when it is clouded over or fogged in, it is there, *you* are there; you are alive at the core. Your consciousness is nothing less than concentrated aliveness.

Now you don't need me to tell you that this core must be drawn into your life as vital energy. You know when you feel contact with that essence, when you experience the warm connectivity and strength that it beams into your life. You know when you make contact with the very root of the self that there is a sense of wholeness and fullness which is absent when that core is obscured because you kicked up too much dust, or wild horses pulled you off course.

The center of your being carries its own signature and when you are aligned with it, you feel empowered and grateful to be you. That's where you want to be, in that state of alignment, when the wind blows down your door, when the hurricane hits.

The more connected you feel to who you are, and are able to locate that charge which ignites in the center of your being, the more you will be able to face whatever Life puts in front of you. That's really the central task that lies before us, before each one of us, to grow and deepen our awareness of this concentrated living essence which has the capacity to align us with our own core. And not only wake us up to who it is we really are but who we can become in those moments when greatness, wisdom or unusual generosity are called for. When destiny calls, we want to be there, and tuned in enough to recognize, '*This is my moment to let myself pour through the veils of hesitancy, doubt or confusion. This is the moment when I know I am really ready to show up.*' There are many things that wake us up to that reality of the inner self, but one important catalyst in our journey of self-discovery is being recognized by others. We can be so grateful to those people in our lives who have *seen* us, not just noticed us, but who saw us at a much deeper level for who it is we really are. They recognized some aspect of our essential truth and they reflected it back to us. They helped call us out of hiding, they invited us to have the courage to show up and be ourselves.

Do you remember when you were that important and magical age 7 being recognized in some special way? Was it a grandparent, or a teacher or a special older friend? Maybe it was only a look, a deep glance into your essence, which conveyed a very clear sense of, *'I see you. You cannot hide from me.'* That sense of being known by others is critical to our development, especially when they really get who it is we are and not who it is we're supposed to be or who it is they would prefer us to be. Be grateful to those who catch a glimpse of your true self! To witness and confirm another person in this way is to participate in a primary form of spiritual communion.

Yet as important as it is to be known by others we must learn, above all else, to know ourselves; *to stand in the truth of the self is to drink the most life-giving force on Earth.*

And as it turns out, stress has a major role to play in leading you ever more vividly into the presence of that truth. The source of your self is an essence of super-saturated awareness which is always attempting to reflect and radiate its influence into every corner of your life, but you get distracted: "*distracted from distraction by distraction*" as the poet T.S. Eliot put it. Pulled into the side-show of one distraction after another, you become accommodated to living in the shadows rather than in the full light of the self. One of the functions of stress is help you see that you are not in alignment with yourself. Stress, as the messenger of the raw energy in the universe, wants to shove you in the direction of your true self. It wants you to taste that elixir of truth you keep hidden even from yourself.

We shut out our own inner voice because we fear it is going to ask too much of us. Marianne Williamson eloquently puts it this way:

"Our deepest fear is not that we are inadequate. Our deepest fear is that we are powerful beyond measure. We ask ourselves who am I to be brilliant, gorgeous, talented, fabulous? Actually who are we Not to be? Your playing small does not serve the world. There is nothing enlightening about shrinking so that other people won't feel insecure around you."

Facing the truth of who you are is only challenging because somewhere along the line you swallowed the *false* notion that you could only become that great soul you longed to be if you were loved and not rejected, if you were given the ideal body and not physically compromised, if you won and didn't lose, or if you got on the A team, got chosen for the star part or you were socially desired. After all were you not conditioned to be one of the winners, to succeed and to have the right answers at school, at home and everywhere you went?

It is phenomenally hard for us to de-condition ourselves from the end-goal reward of the right answer and appreciate the significance of approximate answers, genuine mistakes or differences in perception. For all the time we spend at school, not much of it is dedicated to how we learn. Schools are, in general, enforcers of conformity. The stress to be right, to be part of the in-group, to avoid at all costs being seen as a loser, or to make sure certain people don't know your true feelings, can reflect very real social pressures and it is clear that, for our survival, sometimes we have to go along.

But real learning begins when we cross the stress-line of conformity and step into our own power. Sure, the first thing that may happen is that we stumble, fall, get laughed at, or worse, but the history of human greatness is charted not by ingesting the stress of conforming to such a degree that we kill the spark of our originality, but by *facing the stress which calls us to be who we are in the depth-world of the self.*

At age 16, when he had his first thought experiment, visualizing himself traveling alongside a beam of light, Einstein was so confident about his scientific calling that he left his regular high school without a diploma and applied to a technical school where he could specialize in electrical engineering. Not having a diploma, he had to take an entrance exam, *which he failed.* He then went back to another high school to get his diploma. As an original thinker he found on more than one occasion that he did not click with conventional wisdom or academia. Thank God he kept being willing to move through obstacles and to trust in his own ability to think differently.

Learning how to learn is critical in showing us how to deal with obstacles, roadblocks and dead ends. It is also critical in helping us use and optimize our potentially unique learning style to discover new pathways and set meaningful goals. Learning has its natural challenges and difficulties, and creating a healthy and satisfying relation to its in-built stresses should be the goal of education, mentoring and parenting.

In the direct encounter with stress, we begin to recognize that we cannot move forward until we learn how to relate to obstacles, or anything that impedes or frustrates us from getting where we want to go.

The obstacle is your teacher. Face your teacher.

This is a stance which will ensure some form of conscious and intentional engagement with stress, which is where real learning begins.

Would that we could learn to deeply know ourselves by always being loved, appreciated, admired, welcomed, nurtured in every moment; always taken at our best, and skillfully facilitated to achieve our highest goals. But that is not how we learn and grow is it? *We learn* from engaging what is real; and reality is unpredictable.

We simply do not learn who we are and what we are capable of by things always being the way we would like them to be; or having people always perfectly aligned with our needs and desires. When we try that, we start to avoid reality the way it is, and try to bend it to make it the way we want it to be, which is a recipe for creating really pernicious stress! That is *turning your back* on your teacher.

The truth of who we are emerges out of the contrast of being loved by some and not by others, of finding ourselves embraced by some and ignored by others, of experiencing some of our needs being met and others frustrated, of having some of our greatest expectations met and having others meet with disappointment, of excelling in some things but not in others. Our map of reality is gained by appreciating how both positives and negatives act upon each other, not just by trying to invent a world of false positives.

The truth of who we are needs to be tested in the cross-currents of a complex and multidimensional reality. After all, what would we really discover about ourselves if we were given a free ride? We also know that life would be rather boring if it were always some version of a sunny beach. Of course when we live with the fantasy that it's supposed to be a sunny beach all the time, that's when we discover that medical waste has been dumped in the waters, or the sharks are coming in too close. We don't have to worry about reality giving us a wake-up call. The important thing to remember is that reality is not out to get us—life happens, and since this is so, the important question becomes not only, can we deal with it? But, can we face it and deal with it *honestly*?

The first question that stress asks is, 'What is *true* here?' This is a primary question whose response determines whether we mature or not, and whether or not we advance on the spiritual path.

Stress Wants A Truthful Answer

When your body signals its familiar range of stress alerts, from tightening of the jaw or stiffening neck and shoulder muscles, quickening of the pulse, to tingling little heat bursts of adrenaline in your solar plexus, and on up the scale of messages sent to provoke a speedy response, it is, as we have noted in the last chapter, inviting a clear answer.

Be certain of one thing— if your body doesn't recognize an elemental truth in your response, stress will hang around: '*Don't think you really dealt with that, did you? Aren't those feelings you are having an indication that you really didn't deal with the situation in a clear and up-front way. Who are you trying to fool? Here, let me give you a little bout of anxiety to remind you that you need to address this situation more coherently.*'

The body has this extraordinary capacity to be an antenna for the whole system.

In case you are not convinced: *Try hiding your body's response in a lie detector test. Or now that advanced neuroscience can watch exactly which parts of your brain you are using to process information, do you really want evidence that the body precisely tracks what's going on in your head when you're faking it? How about the analysis and psychological interpretation of your body language? How about the flicker of disdain that can be detected in your eye muscles when the words coming out of your mouth are gushing praise?*

No wonder we talk about feeling the 'prick' of conscience. You've got a little detective agency working in there that keeps the evidence of your transactions even when a part of your conscious mind refuses to admit the truth. You have an in-built BS detector and honest accounting department with long-term memory. How about that? You, in the form of your ego-mind, may have the capacity to override the urgent signals your body produces but ego does not have the power to take over the full assembly of the body's sensitive instrumentation, because ego-mind didn't design it. It comes from millennia of evolutionary experience, which in turn is sourced in a larger cosmos story. The little strutting ego is capable of deceiving itself, but something deeper in us has access to an infinitely larger reality.

You, your body, mind and spirit, are part of an incredibly intricate design, attuned to a harmonic frequency which we might call your *signature truth* or, as Hillman has put it, your *"soul's code."*

When the mind-body experiences that precise ring of truth, it is as if you give it a valid password which gains access to bio-chemical and electromagnetic signals capable of completely re-coding its alerts, advisories and warnings.

Your body has its own very accurate truth-sniffer. Stress hangs around when we try to lie to it, ignore or dismiss it: we bite our nails, we grind our teeth, we get backaches, tension headaches, digestive issues, blood pressure problems and so on. Or it protrudes in behaviors which are not healthy. Our 'issues' get filed by the body's neural circuitry in various parts of the mind-body system as: *'unresolved, needs further attention, still phobic, living in la-la land,' etc.*

Let's face it, we all know that we don't only hide things from *other* people, we have ingenious ways of hiding all kinds of things from *ourselves*. Maybe we don't consider it lying to ourselves when we persistently ignore certain kinds of stress signals—until there is an internal rebellion. We wake up one day and find we just can't tolerate the person we have been sleeping next to for ten years, or that we really hate our job, and we wonder why we put up with it for so long. Well, we lied to ourselves. We ignored our stress responses until they ended up screaming in our face!

As we noted earlier, we have lots of ways to override the body's signals; diffuse them, suppress them or simply ignore them. Any number of circumstances that we meet in the course of a day may require different kinds of responses and split-second reactions. Whatever our response (within the range of relatively normal non-violent responses), if we have an internal response to the in-coming stress which indicates we felt we did our best, and that we responded as appropriately as we could, it will invariably subside. We will have passed our own inner lie detector. So I am not suggesting that you need to micromanage your response to each stress producing event in your life, but I am going to ask you to scrutinize *patterns* in the way you deal with stress.

Let's see if we can get behind your stress profile.

While we all have a repertoire of approaches to stress, and while some of us vary our responses in relation to what provokes or engages us, people tend to develop a characteristic or dominant behavior pattern in dealing with serious stress—they either tend to:

- *internalize it*
- *they push back*
- *they attempt to ignore it*
- *they learn how to engage it.*

Yes, this last approach is the only one that is able to transform negative stress into creative stress.

If your pattern is more to internalize the stress response you may find yourself sucking things up, brooding upon things, quietly seething, holding resentment, feeling grudges, bouts of self-pity and occasional holy martyrdom. You tend to absorb the shock but not release it. At the more extreme end, wounds tend to congregate in you until you break-down, get really ill and appreciate what is needed to heal.

If your pattern is the opposite, you may find yourself vocalizing anger, hostility, lashing out, blaming others and, from time to time, being aggressively self-righteous. You tend to be more armored and re-direct negative energy towards others or other entities, institutions, etc. At the extreme end, you can really hurt others or be abusive until you cross a line and you have need for anger-management or more serious interventions.

If your pattern is to suppress stress signals, you may find yourself engaged in a variety of self-sedation techniques, numbing your feelings or filling your life with so much busyness that you don't have time to deal with the things that are the causal undercurrent of real stress in your life. You tend to deny the reality of stress and can find yourself out of touch with colleagues, family or friends. At the extreme, something dramatic and painful forces you to wake up and see what is real and valuable in your life before it is too late.

If your pattern is to engage stress, you do not flinch from direct encounters with difficult situations. You can be determined to sort things out, reveal your true feelings in awkward or threatening situations, and take unambiguous responsibility for your behaviors. You become a creative problem-solver, innovator and expressive artist. At the extreme, you become an agent for moral leadership, conflict resolution, dialogue and informed choice...and if you keep going, you become a force for healing, selfless service and evolutionary leadership.

It is important to reinforce that there are a wide variety of responses to stress, and while each one of us might have reflected, at different times, some part of the whole spectrum, in general we tend to develop *a pattern* in relation to particular kinds of stress that really get under our skin, or which go right to that place where we have a history of getting aroused, triggered or spun out.

Remember *stress wants a truthful answer* and by that I mean a response which has the capacity to dissolve or transform its energy, not block it off or stockpile it until it has to force you to release it. The body is a very precise barometer of inner conditions of truth; it can register in multiple ways whether

31

or not you are living in integrity with your deeper self. We know that mind and body are profoundly interconnected and interfused. One thing the integrated mind-body system does very well is record patterns of stress.

To help you get a picture of the pattern of stress in your life let's go back and see how you dealt with it from an early age. Let's start with a disappointment. Disappointment brings stress to our door and bitter disappointment delivers intense stress in an express package.

Practice: Visualization and Disappointment

Visualize yourself somewhere between eight and ten years of age—see if you can remember an occasion when you met with disappointment. Maybe it was a gift you were expecting that never came; or a party you were shocked to discover you were not going to be invited to; or a vacation that had to be canceled, or a parent who missed once again your big game or school performance.

Do you remember how you responded—how you choked up?

- *Did you run and hide so that others wouldn't see your feelings?*

- *Did it bring on feelings of sadness and a desire to disengage?*

- *Did it leave you moody?*

- *Did you sulk?*

- *Did you have a tantrum?*

- *Did you go around complaining about the injustice of your situation?*

- *Did you make sure someone was blamed?*

- *Did you resort to snide comments?*

- *Did you take it out on someone else?*

- *Did you find yourself just trying to make the bad feeling go away with the help of candy bars or TV?*

- *Did you find yourself pretending that nothing at all was wrong?*

- *Did you use your disappointment to negotiate filling a different need?*

- *Did you find yourself listening to an inner voice that offered consolation and comfort?*

- *Did you experience relief when you found yourself reaching out to others who were feeling bad for you?*

- *Did you feel bigger having gone through this experience?*

- *Or was it like other disappointments; you just didn't want to talk about them?*

It is not difficult to line up these responses with the categories we identified above: absorbing and internalizing the stress, pushing it away from yourself and finding others to pin it on, suppressing or denying it, or engaging in problem solving and even reaching out to others. So now *trace the pattern,* how did you manage adolescent stresses, stress at work, with regard to family issues, money, intimate relationships, your relationship to social injustice or political conflict? There is a lot of information waiting for us if we can begin to discern our primary or dominant method of dealing, or not dealing, with stress. There is a lot of information, long-stored, for the conscious mind to access and interpret, like a call sustained over time which is finally listened to and answered.

Visualize the following: you meet a mysterious person, you don't know who she is or where she has come from, she just suddenly appears. She stops you in your tracks and tells you that she's going to give you a message of great importance, of supreme importance, which you must take to your best friend's house. She hands you an envelope like no envelope you've ever seen before. It is weighty, expensive and official looking.

As you look at it you can't tell whether it contains good news or bad news. One thing is very clear, whatever is inside this envelope is extremely important. Before she disappears the mysterious lady looks at you with the most penetrating stare as if to remind you that you have been given this very special assignment and that you must do everything in your power to make sure that this highly important letter is delivered to your friend as quickly and as efficiently as possible. And with no further ado, you make your way in great haste to your friend's house. When you get there, you ring the buzzer and can't wait for the door to open so that you can hand over the letter and find out what it's all about.

In case you haven't worked it out yet, the friend delivering you the urgent letter is your stress mechanism, with its mysterious connection to the energy of this sacred universe.

There it is ringing your buzzer, waiting for you to open the door. It rings one more time to let you know it has something important for you to look at. If no one answers the door, your little friend is going to start doing more than ring the buzzer—she's going to start raising her voice and banging the door! And if you only open the door a crack, take the letter with one hand and then close the door without letting her know anything about its contents, you can be certain she's going to hang around and start to wonder what's really going on inside the house. Then she will wait and listen for signs to tell her whether the letter brought good or bad news. And she'll certainly begin to wonder if you're really friends or not. But open the door, come out and share the contents of the letter with her, and even if it's bad news, she will know exactly what is going on, and she will have done the job she came to do and she'll always be your friend!

In other words, a healthy and honest relationship with stress requires a direct encounter with it. When it knocks on your door, it needs to find someone at home. It needs to know that the message has been received and understood. It needs to know the simple truth. It needs to know that you appreciate it is attempting to act in your best interest. Mastering that simple transaction is the basis of psychological maturity and the launch-pad for spiritual growth.

At the heart of this story is the notion that *things come unglued without an open, conscious and responsive core in the center of our being*—without it we cannot activate intention, we cannot find our truth, let alone live from it and manifest it fully.

The first commandment is, 'Be yourself.' It is a commandment that strikes terror in the hearts of many. You might even say it is a primal existential stress none of us can avoid. We wonder, '*Do I really have permission to be myself? How will I be received if I am really myself? Is it safe to be myself? Who am I?*' And sometimes we find ourselves utterly amazed: '*Wow, how did I achieve that? I had no idea I was capable of such things! Where are these incredible ideas and feelings coming from? What is this charged feeling I have about my own destiny? How do I stay true to myself?*'

The truth is we cannot know the answers to many of these questions without getting some feedback from the world around us and from facing or wrestling with some measure of confusion. As it turns out confusion, and the stress that it can produce, is a great ally.

Be grateful that stress brings confusion.

Perhaps the first time you made a choice to directly engage stress, instead of trying to avoid it, was when you really didn't know which way to turn. Sometimes our own games catch up with us, do they not? We brush off a problem until, as Tom Stoppard wryly puts it, "*The skeleton in the closet comes home to roost.*" Or until someone confronts us and we have to look in the mirror. When we are finally called out by friends or circumstances, it can be difficult to face the fact that we have not been entirely honest with ourselves. It can be an acute struggle to admit to ourselves things that we have let slide for a long time. Denial *seems to work*, that's why it can go on for a long time before it is exposed and when it does the game is up: red faces galore!

We pretended to ourselves that our drinking habit was not a problem; that our habit of gossiping about others would not catch up with us; that our penchant for pornographic websites would not be discovered by a member of our family; that our quiet exploitation of a business partner would not be exposed; that our ridicule of a colleague would not come back to haunt us; that our habit of ignoring our kid's antisocial behavior would not have serious consequences, or that our quiet contempt for people less fortunate would not erode the moral high ground we presumed we stood upon. *When the hammer falls* in such situations we can find ourselves in significant distress and even genuinely perplexed about our own behavior. Inevitably, we reach a choice point. We can try to brush things under the carpet, make excuses or simply try blustering our way out of the stress of being exposed. Or we can summon up the courage to see what is really there. And as soon as we do, rather than instant choirs of angels, it can get very confusing for a while.

There are thousands and thousands of ways in which confusion attends stress. *And what compounds our challenge* is our social conditioning to move as fast as we can into solution mode. After all so much of our education focused on having right answers. Remember those days when the hands shot up in the air trying to let teacher see who was the first to have the right answer?

Whether it has been our own behavior that has precipitated the crisis, pressures created by the behavior of others, or tragic circumstances beyond anyone's control, we can easily find ourselves at a loss, and unable to see clearly how to deal effectively with situations which are demanding our response. And the stress piles up in the absence of a coherent plan of action.

So why is confusion an ally?

Confusion is your opportunity to admit that you don't know. Mystics and saints try to hang out in '*I don't know.*' It is a pretty high state. When you begin to surrender to 'I don't know' you break the control that *false certainty* has over your life. Admitting doubt is a dimension of the authentic journey of faith. Mother Teresa, no less, wrote in her journal about her struggle with doubt. And if you progress far enough on the spiritual path you will inevitably experience some version of the dark night of the soul. False certainty is an artificial cocoon out of which no real transformation can occur. Confusion sets the stage for an authentic inquiry into what is going on and it invites you to look at deep levels of causation. When you admit you don't know which way to turn, you could say that the stress pushes you further back, so that you can get a wider perspective. Confusion allows for movement in a new direction whereas absolute certainty can be a kind of treadmill.

Premature certainty stunts your growth!

Stay confused for long enough and you will start to wrestle with those important questions which help you mature and grow:

'How did this happen? How did I get here? What is most needed of me in this moment? Where does my true strength lie? How can I alleviate my own and others' suffering? How can I change my life for the better?'

Confusion is a place where you begin to hold the tension between conflicting needs, and conflicting demands which have been placed upon you. It is where you are free to make a new assessment because the old way of doing things can no longer continue.

Now, maybe, you can begin to see why a direct encounter with stress starts to lift you to higher ground. By engaging it, you open yourself to exploring new meaning in your life. Close to the notion of confusion is another dimension of the direct encounter with stress which is a necessary wrestling with different choices and feeling the tension between them. It might surprise you, but getting inside that tension is an essential ingredient in building your spiritual muscle.

Wrestling with competing truths invites authenticity and creativity, and overcomes the worry mind.

Just as you begin to deepen your relationship with truth and integrity, truth reveals itself to be more than one-dimensional. Truth wilts under platitudes, rigid formulas and unbending codes. It is not difficult for us to appreciate that truth has two faces: one simple, the other complex. As you hone in on what is true for you, it can be resoundingly clear or filled with perplexity. Both are good!

Perplexity forces us to consider the truth from different angles. We can find ourselves in the grip of intense stress simply because we have decided not to make a premature or knee-jerk decision. Yet this is where life-changing experiences occur. When faced with really difficult decisions, if we permit ourselves to live in the tension of competing truths, we are invariably nudged upwards onto higher ground. By this I do not mean that we are given a magic wand to resolve the tension, but, rather, by engaging in a process which catalyzes our deeper values and aligns them with one approach over the other, we stimulate growth and creativity. By bringing more *concentrated attention* to our challenges we are applying fresh resources of conscious energy to help resolve our situation.

There is no one right answer when it comes to: '*Should I move into a retirement community or not? Should I allow a relative to transition or undergo further life-support interventions? Should I take chemotherapy or risk a non-invasive alternative? Should I tell my religiously conservative family about my real sexual orientation? Should I have an abortion? Should I support the war?*' In wrestling with these exacting and stressful decisions, we are asking the fundamental question, '*What is the best way for me to live my truth?*' Keep wrestling with that and the cauldron of intense energy which builds will inevitably ensure that you bring a rich and deep quality of attention to your dilemma. You are now in a potent direct encounter with stress and literally beginning to lift it, and allowing it to be guided by your sincerity, to a place where you will make your own unique and creative choice. Your own higher consciousness will be imprinted on the decision. That is accomplishment!

This does not guarantee that you will make the perfect decision, but it will be the *right* decision for you at that time: and you will recognize the thrill that comes from making a decision which reflects your inner core.

In wrestling to imprint your decision with your truth:

- *You expand your conscious self and reduce the influence of ego.*

- *You create a pathway for further authenticity to flow through you and be tested.*

- *You switch on the light of a more integrated conscience and invite it to stay lit.*

- *You open yourself to fresh insight, the power of imagination and unexpected options.*

If, or when, later, you find you need to make a choice that seems more authentic, wiser or spiritually informed you will have no need to regret past responses but only to see that you have already established a path in your life that is dedicated to growth and self–development. Creative engagement with stress is always about cooperating with *movement* and the current that carries you inexorably to your true self.

When we enact new choices which have strong meaning for us, our body's response is to forge *a new neural pathway* in the brain. Neuroscientists refer to this as the neuroplasticity of the brain. When our choices are affirmed and reinforced, this new wiring actually gains a protective coating called myelin, like the insulation which surrounds electrical wires. We are supported when we direct our attention into direct engagement with our issues and concerns and forge our own destiny: '*Let me get that straight,*' your neurons seem to say, '*You intend to change your lifestyle! And I can see you mean business because you are selling*

*the house, buying a hybrid and rejecting beef as an unsustainable food source. OK, let's
start re-wiring your brain!'*

You may have wrestled long with whether or not these were the right decisions to make, but you knew you had become so unsettled and uneasy about
your lifestyle that something had to give. When this radical alternative presented
itself, it woke you up at night with jolts of fear, and even a little panic. Stress
kicked in, *'Do you really understand the consequences of these decisions? You may
feel good about driving a hybrid but you will feel like a freak at the family Fourth of
July party when you ask if there are any veggie burgers!'* That is what we can call
your neurotic worry mind speaking to you. But you, hopefully, have gone to a
deeper place in making your decisions, a place that emerged out of difficult, but
thoughtful and considered, wrestling with that primary question: *'What is the
best way for me to live my truth?'* When you respond as creatively as you can to
that question, the decisions you make will be an affirmation of your own highest
values not your most neurotic impulses.

Worry mind can build stress with its capacity to invent dire and difficult
scenarios. It will do everything it can to present itself as your voice of reason,
your conscience, your inner guide. It is good at hijacking the stress mechanisms
of your body and cranking them up. Truth is, the worry mind is a fake. Spiritual
teachers will tell you that it is broken. It feeds off a deep illusion that it is real and
everything else is alarmingly false. It is nothing less than *Chief Emissary of Ego*.

How can you distinguish worry mind from the kind of sincere engagement
and wrestling with difficulty we have been discussing? Worry mind is actually a
genius at creating negative stress. It stirs up trouble. It will invariably contradict
itself: *'Do this! No, do that! Better yet, do nothing.'* Worry mind is not interested in
resolution. It plays with stress in order to avoid reality. Remember that we said
that stress is a force of nature, one which is a call which seeks a truthful response.
How do you think it feels when it is captured by a lie, or a pack of lies? Well, as

we have noted, its energy builds like a geyser which eventually bursts through the earth's crust with scorching hot water. Ouch! *'Now show me the truth!'* it declares to the astonishment of the ever-distracted ego-mind.

The direct encounter with stress, which *faces* difficult choices and, at times, gut-wrenching dilemmas, draws the energy upward so that it can engage it more consciously. *Attention* is given to the nature of the dilemma that is before you and *intention* is summoned. Even though the energy may remain difficult and unresolved, an invisible alchemy has already begun to take place. Since the stress is being attended to it is being pulled toward meaning, values, and creative problem solving. As we have noted earlier, one of the signs of this kind of encounter with stress is that often it creates new demands and challenges. The nature of the response is, in biblical parlance, *a girding of the loins.* Energy is summoned, because more energy will be needed as you take action.

In the case of the worry mind you close off, act out of fear, or spin so much you fail to take appropriate action. In the direct encounter you open up, don't force a premature response and find yourself engaged by the energy, and even excitement, of a response that has your true self written all over it!

3

Leading from the Center of Your Being

Most people want to be liked. They also don't like to be seen as complainers. They know that whiners are despised by most people. So it is natural for most of us to put a positive spin on things, it is linked in our minds with putting our best foot forward. Experience tells us from an early age that negative seems to attract negative: people get down on you for grouching when they themselves are out of sorts or don't have the patience to deal with your issues. But smile and people will tend to smile back at you even though they may talk about you behind your back.

We have strong genetically inherited survival needs to be in with the group: we know all too well what happens to those who are isolated by their peer groups and affinity groups. It is highly stressful to be cast out by any social, familial or professional groups, especially when we want to be in.

Rejection sends those stress alerts deep into our emotional and cognitive centers. In case you haven't experienced any significant rejection in your life, these are the kind of stress alerts that can become seriously unpleasant. It is indeed very hard for us to accept rejection or its related family of stressors in the form of betrayal of trust and blind prejudice. The body knows well how dangerous it is for you to be pushed aside and ignored by others. In such situations it may send persistent threat alerts which can precipitate both physiological and psychological problems. Naturally, this is perniciously toxic when you have very little or no control over the conditions or forces causing your exclusion. Whether through your personal experience or through your knowledge of history, you know, or you can appreciate, the painful and destructive results of class, caste, religious, racial and ethnic exclusions. Some people may want to be hermits but nobody wants to be an outcast.

You get the point, we have strong incentives to please others. And anyway, what does it hurt to be nice to others, or to go along with the general mood? No stress there, right? Just accentuate the positive and eliminate the negative, and you and everyone else will feel better. No big deal.

Partner to you: "*How are you feeling?*"

(your partner wants to be sympathetic; feels something is awry)

You to partner: "*Fine.*"

(you do not want to trigger worry which could lead to "*why don't you*" sessions, which feel unhelpful or like being nagged)

You to you: "*How am I feeling? I'm actually feeling heavy and dragged down. I can't get over feeling burdened. No one thing seems to be pulling me down, just a general feeling of being oppressed.*"

Anyone relate to these disconnects?

How do you manage these disconnects say, with your boss, your colleagues at work, your mother or father, your friends, or your neighbors? Clearly you don't want to and don't need to let everyone in on your inner angst. The question is *how thick is the layer of veneer* before you get to those feelings which you don't care to share; and do you yourself even stay in touch with that place?

Practice: Self Observation and Negative Stress

Try a little experiment over the course of a day or two and observe how often you deflect questions or interactions with others; how often you avoid certain topics and how often you deliberately skim the surface rather than allow things to go deeper. If you can, try to notice what we might call the drip, drip, drip of low-grade stress as certain heavier feelings overflow or back-up from your subconscious mind, which get pushed back or ignored.

I guarantee you'll see stress unattended, an almost invisible stress which is trying to communicate but not getting through, or which is the energy behind various moods or physical problems.

So we are not so concerned with any one particular interaction but noticing the pattern which applies a false positive over a territory that feels negative or too difficult to deal with. The reason I call the direct encounter *the first stage* of creative stress is because, in being willing to engage the cause of stress and not merely deal with its effects, consciousness can open up trapped energy and allow it to begin to shift and re-direct the way you look at things. Instead of being a negative, that energy starts to get released in healthy ways and gets channeled into creative action.

The false positive does wonderfully well at telling us that we don't need to attend to our true feelings because they are ugly, unwanted in some way, or that they are going to be too difficult to handle and will end up making people upset with us. In that regard, it is a liar! False positives play for short-term gain and end up with ever diminishing returns until they can no longer suppress the truth. Then, like having termites, you really notice them when the damage starts to get obvious.

Creative stress is all about freeing you to be you: and there is no short-term, quick-fix that is able to deliver you to yourself. There are no shortcuts. The path to your highest self opens up when you commit to exploring your true self. "*Until one is committed*," declares W.H. Murray, "*there is hesitancy, the chance to draw back, always ineffectiveness.*"

So what is the true self one must commit to?

In the spiritual traditions, the *self* is a tiny cocooned version of the Self. The path from the little local *self* to the Self, eventually experienced as oneness in and with an all encompassing Reality, requires shedding the layers of the cocoon. Each compacted layer that must be broken through and left behind is simply something that has obscured the multifaceted nature of the greater Reality. These layers are sometimes referred to as the veils of illusion. They are not so easy to penetrate, and the emerging soul must work at shedding them all.

This process of shedding we call *awakening*. Awakening is accompanied by self-knowledge. Any time we shed an aspect of ourselves which is less than real we grow into a greater awareness of our true self. The true self is the one hatching out of the binds, constrictions and limitations of the cocoon. The force that does not want to face this emergence is sometimes referred to as the false self or ego. The trick here is to appreciate that the true self discovers that it has a higher self which can help guide it through its initiations and challenges. For every move-ment the true self makes towards it, there is a response by the higher self. This is another example of the pervasive nature of call and response in the universe.

The higher self is able to *witness* your level of commitment to growth, and reward your efforts with the kind of enhanced awareness which permits you to see who it is you truly are. Self-knowledge could not be gained without the aid of the witness. So it is a beautiful design really, when you turn away from any force that would help you grow you are feeding yourself less self-awareness. When you turn and face that force and commit to growth, the witness provides you with a mirror in which you feel and see yourself expanding and embracing a larger reality. This is like breathing more oxygen into your lungs for the climb ahead.

Creative stress leaves you energized not depleted. Have you ever been completely exhausted after tackling a heavy problem and yet felt a deep vitality that tells you that you have more strength than you have ever had to deal with challenges? It is the kind of energy that is not exactly physical, it is more psycho-spiritual in nature. It is like discovering an inner wellspring that has mysteriously bubbled up inside you, in response to your willingness to engage that primal call of the universe we call stress.

Leading from the Center of your Being

There are a number of psychological profile tests you can take which will reveal your general predispositions; more introvert/more extrovert, detail/big picture oriented, more led by feeling/more led by thinking, more disposed to analysis/more disposed to synthesis, more auditory/more visual, more verbal/more physical, better at problem solving/better at imaging new approaches. Some are always looking for balance, others looking for the edge; some flower in reverence for tradition, others cannot thrive unless they are breaking new ground. Some express love as the lover wooing the beloved, others as the one who drinks in the lover's attention. Add to these predispositions, your psychological profiles and personality traits, your genetic inheritance, distinct family habits, social status and culturally specific conditioning, and no one person will ever be identical to another.

Now reductionists will argue that we are an amalgam of these elements: take away any one, and you won't have the same person. Scientific reductionism, based on a materially dominated perspective of reality, does not accept the existence of a core identity. They see, at best, a continuity of adaptation, context re-framing and other behavioral and observable phenomena. They have exceptional difficulty with validating subjective experience as anything but a truly amazing by-product of an objective and verifiable matrix of measurable data. Consciousness, they argue, is an epiphenomenon of the brain's bio-chemistry. Fortunately, the materialists have been getting clobbered by the undeniable truth that subjective consciousness is deeply enmeshed in the overall design of reality as we understand it. Physicists peering into the deepest substrate of matter have found that their own observing consciousness is completely inextricable from that which is being observed.

We don't have to delve into the weird world of quantum physics to appreciate that all of human civilization is based upon the creation of meaning: we are meaning makers. We create and destroy worlds based upon our subjective perceptions, our mental models and moral constructs. We live in an ambiance of consciousness which knows itself, its powers and capacities through relationship. Everything in existence is in relationship. Life could not exist without relationships which tune their alignments across the cosmos all the way down to the life of insects, microbes and bacteria. Native peoples remind us:

"Mitakuye Oyasin"—*"All my relations,"* and they mean *all: the rocks, the crystals, the plants, the beings of earth, air and ocean, and every man, woman and child who ever walked upon the face of Earth—we are all related. We are all in relationship.*

Enter you: a subjective witnessing consciousness; a hub of seeing, interpreting and relating. Every aspect of how you relate to the world around you, its

animate and inanimate life forms, and every human you interact with, provides
you with information, feedback and mirroring. You know, through vibration,
when you are in harmony with the life around you; you know when you are
warmly aligned *and you know when you have caused disharmony, when you have
fallen out of alignment or you are being attacked.* In the spiritual traditions, the
one in you who sees your behavior and who discerns whether or not you are
in balance with yourself and others is your soul or the witness. It is the part of
you that is aware that you are conscious. It is even able to see you veer off into
unconscious or murky territory.

When we live consciously in the awakened state of an ever-present witness,
we have reached a very high spiritual state. We will be exploring the development of that state throughout this book. For now, it is critical to appreciate that
we can and we must *cultivate* this locus of conscious awareness in ourselves: the
center of unfolding in our being. There is a place we go when we are looking
to be in resonance with our own best judgment. It is the place we go when we
want insight, direction or when we ache to feel in tune with our own wisdom
and integrity. Some people actually feel this place of alignment as an energy in
the frontal lobes, they lean into it, into the space between the eyebrows where
the third eye is said to be. Others feel that sense of the core self deeper in the
brain and resonating at the top of the head. Others feel a radiant energy in the
center of the chest above the heart or in the heart beat itself. Still others feel it
pulsing strongly from the middle of the solar plexus or even down in the mysterious knowing of the gut and there will be others who feel it carried in the
breath and moving like a refreshing breeze through the body.

*See if you can feel where you draw your 'integrity and insight energy' from. Let's
distinguish integrity and insight energy from 'cognitive concentration energy' 'emotional charge energy' 'fight or flight energy' 'sexual and erotically turned-on energy.'
There is a quality of coolness to this energy, you draw from it, like slaking a thirst.*

You can rest in it because it is an energy which has your signature on it, it is quintes-
sentially you. It is the sweet spot of your deepest intelligence.

This is the place you must cultivate so that it is more than something fleetingly glimpsed or rarely accessed. It is your spiritual home. It is where the witness
resides. As you work with it, you may find that you experience its physical manifestation differently and even experience its location beyond the body. There are
more than enough books about how to pray or meditate and you must choose
whatever path is right for you. Whatever techniques you use to help you hone
in on the center of integrity and insight energy within you, work with them.

When the hammer falls, when circumstances lead you into intense drama
and testing, if you have expanded a deep resonant awareness of that place, it will
be a wellspring of authentic and creative action. When negative stress is pulling
you in conflicting directions, learn to let your response be authored from your
center: not some outer fringe of your more manic, depressed, naïve, fearful or
controlling self. Remember you are a subjective meaning maker. You are also
the receptive channel of everything fresh and original that comes from deep
inside. So when you are tested by life's small and large challenges you will need
to be able to draw upon your greatest creativity which mysteriously unfolds out
of your *own* higher self.

Creative Action

Creative action is the opposite of destructive action. When we are faced
with the multiple forces that can throw us off balance, leave us feeling cornered,
disempowered, wounded or deeply threatened, we are either negatively or creatively aroused. Negative responses include paralysis, action in which we bring
more hurt upon ourselves or words and actions which damage others. We can
find ourselves swamped in self-pity, or provoked into blame, condemnation

and attack. Several of the negative responses may seem like a determined and aggressive way of engaging the source of your problems but, under scrutiny they reflect many of the deflection and override strategies we have explored earlier. They do not deal with root causes and do nothing to help you deal with your default response to stress.

The direct encounter with those forces is not so concerned initially with fending off stress as understanding it. The brilliance of this approach is that it employs the primary resources of consciousness to tackle difficulties and dilemmas and thus, from the outset, invokes your higher self rather than a more instinctively triggered self.

Marshall Rosenberg suggests that if someone is berating you or even acting in a provocatively hostile manner toward you, that you ask them, "*What do you need me to understand?*" While this is not guaranteed to work in every circumstance, this particular method of engaging an angry person in an obviously stressful situation, can short-circuit the other's overloaded emotions by requiring them to explain their need. It can circumvent irrational behavior and open dialogue. "*Do you need me to understand that I have offended you in some way?*"—is a question which invites an affirmative answer. Equally, "*I need you to understand that I have been really hurt by your words*"—is an invitation not to blame, but for you to process what I am saying at a higher level. The creativity which emerges from a direct encounter with such high-stress energy is one that initiates movement towards dialogue and understanding; it becomes the agent of transformation rather than regression.

Destructive action can be avoided by seeking to understand what is causing your stress and why you are reacting to it negatively. Why, when someone else has a got a problem, do we so often let it impinge upon us? Well, we all have hooks in certain areas as long as we are spiritually developing. Maybe only a spiritual master has no hooks left. We literally get roped in by others as they find our hooks. If we didn't have those hooks, the grief, anger, jealousy, and callousness of others would roll off us.

And when we are not hooked we are *free* to respond compassionately and creatively.

To find your hooks is not difficult:

Think of the last time you got triggered. First, what was the nature of the trigger? Was it around feeling betrayed? Was it some aspect of perceived injustice? Was it a feeling of getting picked on or dumped on? Was it around someone else's mistakes, inefficiency or slacking off?

Whatever form the trigger takes, it doesn't just one day show up, you can be sure that the hook is formed through a *pattern* of experience.

Let me share one of those patterns in my own life. One that began in the womb!

It seems that I was conceived on the eve of my sister's death. She had been paralyzed for long months after falling down the granite steps leading to her school. She had broken her spine and developed spinal meningitis. On 11/11/1950, she left her body. By January, my mother realized she was pregnant: a child lost, a child given. As I formed in her body, there is no doubt that I experienced her profound suffering and loss but I was powerless to crawl up inside her heart to ease her pain. A pattern began even in this embryonic stage of my development.

Although I was happy as a child, I had certain insecurities: one was a feeling of loss and sadness whenever my mother left the house and the other was a feeling at night when the light was off, and my bedroom was darkened, that something threatening was there. It was a fear that gained power by being shadowy and undefined. My mother had once told me my birth was difficult: she had to struggle to let me take in life only to potentially have it prematurely robbed. Somehow there was a primal fear which we shared, that forces beyond our control—which could be experienced as threatening and malevolent—could snatch you up and take you away.

So how do I get hooked? I am good at confronting challenge but if I intuit that someone is not being straight with me, if I sense manipulation, sneakiness, or inexplicable betrayal, I get hooked. It is what I call the lump under the carpet syndrome. I am most at ease when things are brought out into the open, when whatever has been hidden as a grudge or difference of opinion is shared. Because I can quickly sense when someone holds something against me or is just plain dishonest does not mean that there is always a way to confront the truth. So to overcome this trigger, when I feel unease or off-balance in those settings, I must allow myself to be in my full and optimal state of creative engagement *despite* assorted lumps under the carpet—which I have now developed quite an antenna and expert eye for. I can tell you it has not been easy to learn equanimity, even as you see subtle threads of manipulation spun around you. Learning to rise above is a tall order and, for many of us, our life's work.

To first observe, and then transcend, one's own trigger patterns is not only learning how to transform negative stress, it also is to walk the path of spiritual self-liberation. The field of limitless creative action awaits those who first deal with their own stuff before tackling other people's issues.

Now I am not suggesting that everything which triggers you is merely your projection. There *are* malevolent forces in the world, there are mean-spirited people, there are injustices and there is exploitation and oppression. But as long as they hook you, they will tend to generate a negative mental and emotional circuitry which will keep you off-balance. Think of a being as liberated and as effective as Mahatma Gandhi. In taking on the rank oppression of the British Empire in India he never became like them. He never resorted to violent or demeaning attacks. He masterfully took on himself a lifestyle that epitomized his values, not theirs. He denied himself food as a method of protest which only increased his reputation and power. He revealed the power of example and spiritual intention as no other individual in the 20*th* century. Yet he never flinched from direct encounters with his oppressors. He engaged them par excellence with creative action designed to free India from their rule.

It may not be your destiny to send an empire packing, but we live lives of action, and the sphere of our engagement with the world moves out in concentric circles from self to others, from family to community, from local to national, from national to global. These are times which call for the optimal creative involvement of every citizen of planet Earth in re-making our world so that it is more peaceful, compassionate and sustainable. This work always begins close to home and is graphically revealed in how we walk our talk; how we deal with the needs of family members; how we serve the health and welfare of citizens; how we invest in our own communities; how consciously we consume and abstain from consumption; how we protect minorities; and how we honor and celebrate cultural differences.

This is not work for others to do, this is your work. For the world is re-created through creative change in the home, the workplace and in the greater community, the world over. Never has it been more true that each one of us is called to be a conscious actor in a revolution that begins in our own consciousness and radiates out into the world, creating the shift that will transform the root causes of the destructive spirals of negative stress that now threaten our collective health and prosperity, and the survival of our planet.

But don't expect that when you engage in a direct encounter with a stressed world, leading from your center and opening the channels of creative action, that you will not meet with resistance, testing and lots of obstacles to surmount. If rejection triggers you, you will need to work on that before offering yourself as a creative change agent in the world.

This is when your direct encounter with stress clearly becomes spiritual work: when you can transcend being rejected. History is replete with examples of people who appeared to have been great losers, only to eventually be recognized as the true leaders of evolutionary momentum and achievement. Great scholars, saints, artists, scientists and political reformers have been ignored, ridiculed, beheaded, tortured, locked in prison for years, sent into exile or have died in poverty and obscurity. Again and again they selflessly passed on to future generations their gifts of insight, ingenuity and wisdom. Without their tenacity and courage humanity would be captive to bigotry, superstition, slavery and oppression.

Well we may be getting ahead of ourselves. To have the capacity to endure what our greatest moral leaders endured requires a little more than the ability to engage directly, consciously, truthfully and skillfully with what comes to us in the form of challenge and stress—it requires an ability to ultimately embrace what it is we are given to do, and to walk through the fire of fear and doubt until we manifest the fullness of our soul's truth. Between the first authentic encounters with stress as our teacher, and the complete surrender to inner truth, there is a critical stage in the journey to our highest self, which is that amazing time of growth in our lives when we deeply befriend the teacher, our soul's initiator, in the form of what is given, and whatever is given. It begins with a handshake. And a deep bow of gratitude for the life we have been given.

My own life experience has carried me into the most treacherous and difficult places where people are exposed to ultimate stresses and unimaginable suffering. What has always moved me is not that people can break under such conditions but that they can also become beacons of evolutionary capacity. Here are two stories of extremely negative stress in the cauldron of intense challenge; one where stress insidiously breaks the person's spirit, the other where the spirit triumphs.

Beirut and the Torture Slab

Let's face it: none of us really knows how we would respond to extreme stress when faced with the murder of a relative, losing everything in a catastrophic act of nature such as a hurricane or fire; being raped, kidnapped or tortured; living under military occupation or in conditions of severe poverty, exploitation and disease. Yet these things happen. It is important to face the truth of their existence and to do all in our power to create a healthier, more equitable, more peaceful and sustainable planet. I can only share with you two stories from my own experience which reveal how extreme stress can, on the one hand, insidiously penetrate and sear the psyche creating life-long distortion and trauma, and, on the other, reveal our nobility and confirm our more exalted nature as conscious and spiritual beings.

The first story comes from a period when I was living in Beirut. It was 1983; we had been through a war in which the Israeli army had entered Lebanon and bombed Beirut in an effort to dislodge the Palestinian Liberation Organization and its leader, Arafat. Civilian casualties were high. Eventually the PLO agreed to leave. But the assassination of the newly installed Lebanese President was used as a pretext for the Israeli occupation of West Beirut. Shortly after, Lebanese militias, tacitly abetted by the occupying army, committed the brutal massacre of men, women, children and babies at the Sabra Chatilla refugee camp.

Not long after the Israelis had departed, and before further internecine communal fighting broke out in Lebanon, I found myself in conversation with a sixteen year old young man in my local grocery store in West Beirut. I expected to find him relieved that the war was over but grieving, as most people were, the terrible loss of life and the almost unbearable pall of suffering that weighed down those who had seen and endured the depravities of brutal violence. Not so, he was deeply depressed for ther reasons.

55

He was depressed because the war had been a time when his life had taken on *intense excitement and meaning.* You see, during the war he felt he had been somebody special, now he was just a grocery store boy. During the conflict he had helped foreign journalists get around, took them to PLO bunkers to get interviews, showed them apartment buildings that had been bombed, assisted medical crews in locating places where they could perform urgent medical care and even surgery. He knew how to get around and where to go if a ceasefire broke down. I saw how he had lived the famous adrenaline high of war, how he had lived through the horror by creating a movie and adventure based on his own remarkable audacity. But the movie was over, and reality was slowly settling in with its inescapably chilling truth: a truth that would inexorably take hold of his psyche and leave him wounded and betrayed for years to come.

The saddest truth of this young man's war-time experience was that he had been able to conquer the stress of extreme danger and thrive off the power it gave him, but he couldn't endure the stress of a return to normality.

I have no words to express the pain I have witnessed in those whose lives have been shattered, in both graphic and hidden ways, by extreme violence. My own response to all that I saw in Beirut was to join Amnesty International and to spend ten years of my life as the Director of its Washington Office. It was during that time that I met Juan Carlos Rodriguez. His was also a story of the most extreme stress a human can endure—but one with a different ending.

Juan Carlos was a labor organizer who had been imprisoned and tortured in Argentina during the period of the military junta. I sometimes see an image in my mind of Juan Carlos on a torture slab with men applying electric shocks to his convulsing body.

In one such scene the torture and the pain is so extreme, so finally unbearable, that he fears he will die—and he has this thought: *"I hope that my son will learn that his father died nobly, in a noble cause."* There, in the place where the torturer's work was to go far beyond humiliating him, to reducing him to something less than human—there, in that place, he reaches inside to affirm the nobility of his soul's purpose. In that place of obscene cruelty he defies every attempt to break his spirit. In fact, he becomes the embodiment of the indestructible essence of truth and beauty which reside in the human soul. He did not die that day.

He was finally moved to a prison cell where he was allowed to begin to recover. The days of the junta were numbered, they did not want him released bearing such fresh scars of torture. Eventually, as international pressure escalated, conditions improved. He was allowed access to paper and some crayons. It was there in prison that he drew a set of naive images for his son, who had been born while Juan Carlos was in prison. Amnesty International later published a calendar with those images called, "*Colors of Hope.*" Juan Carlos, brutalized in the ugliest of places a person can be brought to, chose to journey to his own inner child to portray scenes of a world in which innocence, kindness, playfulness and love are the context in which reality is framed and life is supported. He did so, not as a way to manipulate the truth for his son, but as a way to reflect a more primary and original truth.

To Juan Carlos, and all those countless men and women who face the ultimate testing to stare down oppression and offer the world moral leadership and indestructible conscience, I bow to you in deep humility and gratitude. Only through your example can I dare to imagine a world where the worst can be transformed and creativity can emerge from the darkest dungeons. And to those who crack and break under the strain, in whatever form stress enters their lives, may they find healing.

. level two .

the handshake

4

Going All the Way to Uncover the Essential Self

Have you ever been through a really grinding experience, and at the end of it not so much breathed a sigh of relief, as felt a mysterious well-spring of satisfaction? Have you ever found yourself exhausted after going through a particularly challenging period of testing and yet be quite exhilarated at the same time, as though you had learned a new skill, like learning to fly? Or have you experienced that moment when the bitter and the sweet flow into each other so that you can't distinguish one from the other, like those times when the tears and the laughter become one?

These states are all significant indicators of a shift upwards towards greater integration and mastery on your journey. You are no longer playing games with stressful challenges, and repressing or ignoring them, but you have learned how to face them in ways that allow your most authentic self to surface. It is as if that more essential and authentic you has been given a more permanent seat at the table. You don't have to wrestle so hard to bring it to the surface or engage it when stress knocks at your door. You feel the presence of an energy which wishes to engage with life when things get hard rather than withdrawing, or burying your head in the sand.

You are on the brink of changing your whole relationship to stress. You may feel as if you are experiencing the first crocus of spring after a long hard winter. There is a fragility to this movement on the inner plane: '*How do I know it will last?*' you ask yourself. '*Will this new strength endure?*' '*Will I be able to face the next test with such equanimity?*'

You start to look for, or you are given, small confirmations. Someone unexpectedly affirms that you are more present, loving, empathic, kind, compassionate, or supportive. You feel this and other forms of recognition are welcome signs from this deeper reality you are getting to know better.

You also have a sense of self-affirmation when you have found your true center and acted from there. You notice how qualitatively different it is from an affirmation of the ego-self. In fact, a little freedom from ego-dominated mind helps you locate more easily the part of your being which is truly free. This is a little taste of the state of liberation. It is like a cool breeze which can be felt only fleetingly at first. Whatever the sensory or perceptual experience which you derive from having led from the authentic self, at this phase, you are not fully anchored there. You have experienced a state which is, as yet, nowhere near stabilizing into a permanent condition.

But here, at least, the stance we symbolize as the handshake is one that can be portrayed as *willingness*. You are willing to face testing. You know that the negative potential of stress energy can be transformed into learning and growth. You bow to your teacher, '*I am ready to be stretched some more. I see that only creativity can flow from this willingness to face whatever obstacles are put in my path.'*

And, invariably, those obstacles, with the assistance of external stimulus or shock, come from our own stuff. Part of the journey now will be to see more and more clearly *how your own stuff gets entangled with stress* and how to keep transforming that energy when it starts to get stuck or spiral in negative ways. Even though you could argue before a court of law that it is startlingly clear that the things that have been thrown at you were not self-created—and you will do so in your head a thousand times—*you will gradually begin to see* that voice in your head only convenes when it is trying to prove that it is not your stuff but external phenomena which are the cause of your problems, your angst, and negative stress. At this phase, even though you have good intentions, you are still getting snookered by roadblocks and obstacles of your own making which you perceive as coming from somewhere else. At times you are in the flow of synchronicity and affirmation and at other times you are in a place where the gears jam, where things are disconnected and you get zapped.

Creativity Flowing—Creativity Blocked

What are the times in recent months when you have really felt the presence of creative flow in your life?

Maybe for some of you it has been a period of continuous flow—work, home, relationships are all carried in a current of creative energy. It is a time of grace. The quality of your inner life, your intimate relationships, your professional life, all seem to act synergistically. You seem to master every negative possibility and transform it into positive energy or at least not tangle with it in detrimental ways.

Maybe it is not quite that good— your career has really taken off and is currently so fulfilling that you are riding a high that you carry into the part of your life where things might be stuck in a rut without this boost. Success is carrying you over what otherwise might be energy draining chasms.

Maybe you're in the glow of a new relationship, or the birth of a child, and it gives you the kind of motivation you need to get through the tedium of office politics or other frustrations which would otherwise be bearing down on you. With enough love in your life you can face anything, right?

Maybe you're just getting by, living at a level of integrity and commitment, but only experiencing very infrequent creative flow anywhere in your life. You know that life has its contractions and you're living through this one without a lot of drama.

Maybe this is one of those times when things are really hard. You feel like Sisyphus: life just seems to give you one boulder after another to clear. You know something has got to change really soon or you will be in serious trouble.

Let's stay with the upper ranges of creative flow for the moment. What are some of its ingredients?

- *You have a positive self-concept.*

- *You feel alignment and attunement with self.*

- *You experience yourself as generative.*

- *Your energy is in high-performance mode and when stress comes you respond quickly and skillfully.*

- *You feel pulsed by a similar kind of radiant energy, as when you are in love.*

- *In every situation you lead from an expanded, not a contracted, sense of self.*

- *You feel an instinctive affirmation and gratitude that life is flowing for you.*

- *The entropic pull of issues in your past, and the things they trigger in you, has been neutralized You are not easily hooked.*

- *Your attention is absorbed in a current of life-affirming energy.*

- *You feel empowered to extend more warmth and generosity to others and it comes back to reinforce a warmth and generosity towards you.*

- *You understand what one mystic referred to as "the law of reciprocal maintenance."*

- *You are in a flow of giving and receiving at many levels. The little demon of, "I don't deserve it." has taken a permanent vacation.*

Try to sense where you are in relation to this state of creative integration and flow in your life. Draw a line with creativity blocked at one end and creativity flowing at the other end. Where are you along the continuum? Is it easier for you to break up this exercise into categories: professional, personal, family, social, spiritual and political? What do you learn from the contrasts? Does it help you see where you have unblocking to do? Where negative stress is hanging out? Can you do a little homework assignment and—just as you looked back at how you get triggered—see if you can find a pattern for periods of creative flow?

You may find that the greatest flow was not necessarily when the things you had fantasized about, such as the car or the star part, came closer to being a reality, but when you discovered—to your surprise—who you were and what you were capable of. It was the flow that came from a much deeper act of compassion or generosity than you expected of yourself; a moment of courage that lit a candle to your inner nature and its reservoirs of strength; a shift in attitude that rippled through almost every relationship in your life; an idea that came unbidden that stirred your intellect to new heights of curiosity; a deep connection with a mysterious person that ignited your imagination; or when you released resentment and offered heartfelt forgiveness to someone who had transgressed. In each instance, the flow had a cascading effect that pulled you into the river of your own wholeness. It was as if one small part of you helped you remove the blinders long enough to catch a glimpse of *a being destined for oceanic depth* who had been hanging out in an oversized puddle along a dried-up creek. These moments when you are picked up and carried towards the seemingly infinite reserves of essence are a reminder that the truly great adventure in your life is the fullest realization of your inner wholeness and where *it* wants to take you.

The Hindus call this energy flow *shakti*. Learn to cooperate with it and it will take you all the way. As much flow—or shakti—as you feel, you will have times when you find yourself stuck in an eddy or marooned on a bank wondering how you lost the current and how you get back in. You see that the journey of self-realization cannot continue without your conscious cooperation, and that means surrendering to the testing that will be uniquely designed for your soul's progress. The concept I am calling the handshake with stress is all about that inflection point when we have been carried along and really tasted what it is like to be creatively fulfilled—when we are able to recognize and confirm how creative flow comes from the way we deal with our challenges, even when the wind abruptly changes and we find that we have more to learn. It is then we know deep in our hearts that we are going to go as far as we can in this lifetime to *clear out the old stuff* and *reach towards our highest self.* It is that precise moment when we decide to grasp the nettle and not slide back into old patterns that we choose to facilitate our own higher creativity rather than obstruct it. It is the moment, essential in our spiritual development, when we decide to cooperate with the Mystery and not fight it.

As it turns out, this is not a quick lesson by any means.

Getting Back in the Flow

"How are you doing?" —after recent buzz-saw encounter with stress: your car accident, death of a friend, a period of illness,

hurricane devastation to your home, *"Not bad, doing my best to get back in the flow."*

We can recognize people who have changed their relationship to stress from resistance to something more positive. We notice how they come back from difficult and trying experiences with a kind of resilient hope and faith. They are not the complainers. They are not the tedious martyrs. They are not the fakers who feel they must cover everything with a veneer of positive. Their faces may carry deeper lines or furrows but there is greater depth and wisdom present also. Their eyes may show traces of grief or wounding but there is a mysterious light in them which conveys the knowledge that, as one mystic put it, *"all shall be well and all manner of things shall be well."* They carry a smile that comes through the heart rather than across the lips. You can see they may be having some serious difficulty or enduring real testing but they have summoned deeper resources to get them back in the flow.

What is taking shape on the inner plane is the emergence of *higher will* flowing to the conscious mind and activating greater purposefulness. Any coach, whether a professional life coach, a horse riding instructor or football coach, knows that disappointments and defeats can be the turning point: they either catalyze the will or they stunt it. Yet when life wallops you with an unexpected two-by-four it is often a lot more complicated than getting back up on your horse after a fall. There may be no horse. You may find you have no friends to rely on; no loving home to return to; no one who really saw what happened from your perspective. Most of our more soul-testing moments are like this: in some crucial time or decision, we find ourselves alone. What is needed must come from us at precisely the moment we are deeply compromised.

Probably a whole book could be written about this moment—when we feel the mid-point of a vortex of intense emotions pulling us back towards defensiveness or prompting us to move forward in the direction of hard choices, which will, one way or the other, force us to grow. The difference between the direct encounter and the handshake, in the context of this existential choice-point, can be conveyed in the following analogy:

Somehow your true self or your highest self finds itself inside a fortress. The fortress was built in a haphazard way based upon how you dealt with stress. If you learned to avoid certain people or threatening situations because you couldn't handle them, you built walls and blocked entrance to them. If they really freaked you out, you filled your turrets with burning oil to dump on approaching enemies. So your fortress only has doors and passages where you feel secure you can handle things: access is granted where you feel safe and secure. Everyone's fort is different based on their experience and predispositions. But initially for everyone the game is *defend and protect* the fortress of what we perceive is the true self.

In the direct encounter, you make a life-changing decision: there is one particular threat that you feel you can meet face to face and you courageously leave the fortress to do so. To your great surprise you discover that *your true self comes with you—it is not confined to the fortress!* This gives you the strength and courage to leave the fortress more often and encounter other stressful challenges as you learn to overcome your deepest fears.

In the handshake, you enter a new phase of your development. You begin to see how the fortress itself is oppressive: there are too many heavy and thick walls, not enough light, and a dungeon or two where there are still a few prisoners who need to be freed. You see that your task is to begin to dismantle the fortress. And you know that you have your work cut out, but that there is nothing of greater importance now than shedding your own defensiveness. In fact, there is nothing more exciting!

Getting back in the flow in this sense is listening to the call of your soul— calling you back to your true work. And somewhere inside you is a river that can no longer resist the pull to find the ocean. Even when you know that the rapids lie ahead!

Creativity Comes from Subtle Attunement

Whatever you do in life, your creative edge comes from an ability to sensitize and focus your attunement in certain areas. We think of painters, poets, philosophers and cosmologists as tuning into subtle domains and bringing back insights and ideas never before imagined or understood. But any creative involvement is an act of attunement, in reality the accountant is one who appreciates the subtleties of financial transactions; the good parent is one who is subtly attuned to the inner life of the child; the physician to the needs of her patients and the teacher to the hidden capacities of his students. We are fulfilled when we are able to practice these gifts or acquired skills. We recognize a particular quality of flow when we are really tuning into subtler aspects of our work, calling or hobbies. And we are all generally aware when we are not in that subtler attunement and flow. We can perceive the relative flatness of the more humdrum aspects of our life, or the feeling of more fragmentation on the surface, when we come up from deeper experiences of connectivity and flow. When we have spent just a little time in the subtle realm we see all too clearly how frazzled we feel when we get pulled into the hyper-acceleration of modern life or find ourselves juggling too many priorities competing for our attention.

Advanced spiritual work is about increasing the quotient of subtle attention and carrying that attunement into more and more aspects of your life. What becomes apparent as you take on this work is that *you have to begin to deal with your stress-avoidant ego.*

Let's face it, the ego is not subtle: it is a blunt instrument. It is going to block things it believes will be unpleasant for you or which will cast you in a negative light. In the interests of keeping a lid on things and managing your presentation to the world, it tries to minimize *the small still voice* within you which may pull you out of the mainstream or de-rail the prize or promotion ahead. It will attempt to close off inconvenient questions, doubts or subtle intuitions if they are going to disrupt what appear to be obvious and immediate pay-offs and rewards. Ego is a paranoid night watchman of control, moving about your psyche with its suspicious beam of light, looking for intruders or spoilers in the form of inner moral conflict, dreams that go beyond conventional aspiration and longings for wholeness which may involve going through the fire of purification. '*Got to make things look normal, even keel, on-track, eh?*' Ego is not given the powers of discernment of your higher mind or conscience and so it is incapable of taking a more visionary perspective.

Don't look to the egoic mind for clarity or *consistency*: look for narrow self-interest, snap decisions and anything that will suppress confusion, questioning or stress. Consider the occasions when your mind, captured by ego concerns, guilt tripped you for not putting others' needs above your own and then flew into a rage because you couldn't get your own way on something; or how you felt inner scolding when you agreed to follow some more conservative advice that may have dampened the possibility of fun and pleasure and on another occasion felt rebuked by that inner voice when you defied conventional wisdom and went to the beat of your own drummer. Or have you noticed how you defy your own better nature at times: the part of you that says you need to be more generous is frozen out by the part of you that is tight-fisted; the part of you that attempts to keep your thoughts pure is seduced by the part of you that drops into lust; the part of you that wants to save is incapacitated by the part of you that keeps spending; the part of you that is generous and forgiving is shut down by the part of you that shows up as more callous and mean-spirited; the part of you that desires to be more spiritual and contemplative is pushed aside by the part of you that is more distracted and materialistic.

Ego tries to make sure all this gets covered over in the twinkling of an eye. If you really tuned in to inner conflict, your ego would lose some of its important *raison d'etre*—which is control: *'Hey what's going on here? You can't just change your mind because you have a gut feeling, people will laugh at you.'*

Who wants a stress-free life? Your ego!

By now you will hopefully agree, stress is anything but the problem, it is the force which will stimulate your growth or its opposite, a state of ego-cocooned stasis or regression. This cocoon invites you to live the *fantasy* of an exciting and interesting life, but only by shedding the cocoon, or the fortress of the conditioned mind, can you taste an incomparably greater *reality*.

As we learn to recognize the contrast between higher mind and conditioned mind, we see that one is blunt, and the other is subtle. One is mostly uni-directional and mechanistic: *'What is the easiest, fastest, least painful way for me to get it?'* The other is more nuanced, more dimensional and more expansive: *'What do I long for and value most, what am I willing to undergo to find it?'*

So the next time you notice that you just sped through an internal stop sign in order not to have to deal with some discomfort or you pushed back some perplexingly mysterious energy because you sensed that dealing with it could open Pandora's box, just notice what is going on. Falling back into the observer or witness within you is guaranteed to open you up to the subtle dimensions of awareness itself. Watch the part of your energy that is trying to skate past, and navigate around, difficulties and challenges. Look for what we referred to earlier as your default response to stress. You don't have to rush to fix anything, rather, zoom out the lens of your internal camera to see more. Get a bigger perspective. In the analogy of the fortress, you can now feel the energy that lies behind doors you have kept closed; you traverse passageways that were formerly hidden or which you were scared to go down. In other words you are now ready and willing to get to know yourself, the inner territory of the self, as never before. You finally have more than a casual interest in exploring your inner world, you see the, *'Stay out! Don't go there!'* signs but know that you have to take a courageous and compassionate look at whatever it is you fear, avoid, repress or are ashamed of.

And running for the bulldozer when you see stuff in there that is not to your liking is not what is going to dissolve closets or dungeons of negative and toxic energy that have not ever been truthfully faced. No, you will need a much subtler instrument: it is called self-acceptance. Self-acceptance, as it turns out, simultaneously dissolves ego and its great ally, self-doubt.

Self-Acceptance

It can be depressing to look at how much damage we do to ourselves, and to others, from ignoring the things we find difficult or just don't know how to go about contemplating in ourselves. There are closets we fear to open with *issues* inside them. We hope and pray that if we just leave them, they will go away. But they rarely go away. They hang in the background and literally have their own circuitry in the brain. They become a force field which we tiptoe around and they impinge upon our freedom and creativity. Open those closets and you may find that jars containing bottled up negative stress are seeping out like a chemistry project gone wrong. And the catalytic agent, often buried deep in our long-term memory, is a corrosive lack of self-acceptance.

The things that trigger us, as we have noted, can create such deep ruts that considerable energy is needed to transcend them. Before you begin your course correction and launch your internal reform and clean-up campaigns, start your yoga class, or run off to a therapist, I invite you to meditate upon this idea of self-acceptance.

The first thing to notice is that this is a topic with layers to it, like an archeological dig. Your *quick-to-smooth-over-any-issue* ego mind is going to reject any notion that there is anything worth examining. "*I love myself. I accept myself the way I am. I am the way I want to be*"—it says cutely, as it hurtles past those closet doors. After all, if it examined the contents of those areas, it would be less than perfect in the mirror of its own superficial evaluation. If you practice affirmations like the set of words above, you might want to consider where within yourself the affirmation is being made.

Rule number one for opening those closets, which is a rule as ancient as the *Vedas*: *you are not the contents of your consciousness. You are the one who sees.* So even if it stinks, *you* are not what stinks. *That stench is from old stuff you didn't know how to deal with.* It is not you. You are the one who witnesses, who beholds the bad energy, the nasty memories, the hurt feelings, sordid episode, shocking experience or whatever really stressed you out that has been held there and left as evidence of your unacceptability. Because it is so vivid you find you merge with what you're looking at and your tendency is to re-live the experience. Scientists know how heightened emotional experience and shock does in fact imprint long-term memory, but you are not the memory, you are the one who remembers. There is a big difference. One is being *caught* inside a particular feeling that acts as a vortex where trapped energy spins and creates negative stress, the other is *seeing* and recognizing the core nature and *origins* of that feeling and, by so doing, beginning to liberate it for healing and creativity. Ironically, the true gold of radiant, positive and creative energy is right behind the assorted barricades ego erects.

Never has it been so clear—from the insights of psychology, neuroscience and spirituality that we can use our consciousness to liberate ourselves from the prisons that mind and ego create. Consciousness can witness its own reality. It can look upon itself and reveal essence.

There are plenty of books and teachings available on how to develop a conscious witnessing capacity so that, as Michael Singer teaches in *The Untethered Soul*, one has the ultimate goal of never having one's consciousness pulled away by stress-inducing events but have it remain firmly seated in the witness. I invite you to learn how to employ the witness, the capacity of your own deeper awareness to observe the contents of your consciousness, to bring you to an experience of self–acceptance. The witness will transform negative stress and help you tap into freshly charged creative energy.

If I could hold your attention for a moment and impress upon you that deep self-acceptance is about a thorough energy refresh: equivalent to a body detox. It is like bathing in a pristine high mountain stream. This is the cleanse which takes stuck and trapped energy and releases it upwards to subtler and freer creativity in thought, feeling, word and deed. It affirms the root of all positivity in your being.

The blocked energy of negative stress which takes the form of lack of self-acceptance feeds neurosis. Notice how we create dead-ends by *fixating* on where we are unskillful or inadequate. In its extreme form lack of self-acceptance grinds us into a guilty pulp without generating resolution or creative movement:

'I am responsible for where things went wrong in the relationship. I screwed up badly. I cursed them when I should have blessed them. If only I hadn't said that. I really was contemptible in the way I exploited the situation for my own self-interest. I have sinned deeply and the sin can never be erased. They can't see my ugly side, but I can. I can never overcome this hatred. I will never forgive myself. If only they knew how much I loathe the fact that my body is less alluring than theirs.

This kind of self-accusation energy gets stuffed back into the recesses of the brain-mind-body where it is stored and labeled with its own biochemical

73

address. All you have to do is trigger the circuitry of recall , or have someone innocently step on the trip wire which sets it off, and your body will ignite the precise cocktail mix of fear, loathing, disgust, rage, regret, frustration, sadness, alienation or whatever combination of feelings registers the degree of rejection being experienced. These episodes do not necessarily get played out, they most certainly can, but often they will remain internalized and be experienced as mood swings or as swift lightning flashes on the inner screen of the mind without a full blown storm. As noted above, the more the witness is cultivated, the more it will see this trapped energy and appreciate that if it is not transformed it is only a matter of time before the storm eventually erupts and the stress energy forces you to look at yourself more deeply.

So how does self-acceptance begin to re-frame all this?

It unravels a particularly tight knot, or string of knots, which bind the energy and restrict it from flowing. All of these knots form from '*something wasn't the way it was supposed to be.*' Because if it hadn't been that way…well you have quite a story about that don't you? Just locate one of those, '*if only it had been this way instead of that*' and play out in your mind the fantasy you tell yourself about how things might have been different. It doesn't take long for you to see that as much longing as you put into it, the fantasy goes nowhere other than to produce the stress that comes from feeling unfulfilled. It goes nowhere because it didn't turn out that way. You can't change that. This is a familiar teaching to anyone who has studied contemporary teachers like Eckhart Tolle, or the great lineage of teachings through the ages that point clearly at the suffering which is created by attempting to make something be that which it is not rather than *recognizing* what it is.

In fact *the great alchemical power of self-acceptance* is that it restores a truthful and accurate recognition of the ways things are, or were, and in so doing moves a freight load of energy which had covered over the truth with a fiction. Maybe you are getting clearer that the fiction arises solely out of ego concerns and stress avoidance. But let me advise, self-acceptance is minimally significant to you as a concept, until it is practiced. Our goal is the transformation of energy, not the easiest, most relaxing way forward. I want you to experience the creative rush of energy that was stored as negative stress which, in being liberated, now has the power to lift you more deeply into who it is you are as a unique spiritual force and creative agency on this planet. Remember that opening up invites more energy to flow through you. What we are looking at is, instead of asking it to go to the land of your fictions, that you permit it to lift you beyond the confining limits of your ego until it takes you to the really dazzling challenges of a great soul.

Practice: "The Seat of the Witness"

We begin with tuning into the witness. You can do this by watching your thoughts and noticing the ones you get caught up in and the ones that just float by. Some you touch, some you tangle with, others have no freight, no charge. The *charge* exists where there is trapped energy and where you have an issue. You are going to allow yourself to go into charged territory where a swirling vortex of energy can unseat the witness. It's like one of those amusement park games, in this case it is, *Unseat the Witness.* If you succumb to the little cyclones of energy, you get dunked into your issues and you are back where you started. If the witness remains firmly implanted in awareness, you will be carried to a place of deeper observation, which is where you want to go and where you will gain fresh insight!

Are you seated in the witness? Let's travel now to a real energy knot where you know you have charge and watch the voice get more shrill as you approach the heart of the cyclone. Has the stress taken on a voice that is *accusatory, aggrieved, recriminating, melancholic, whining, defensive, sanctimonious*? The way through this energy field is to *tune into* it but not *give into* it and certainly

75

not to block it out. What you are doing through the witness is opening, but going beyond the line of argument that you hear or feel, until you catch the *signature essence* of that tone or vibration. The witness is not a cognitive function of the brain sent to sort things out and fix problems. *First*, you are dealing with an energy knot created in the past, you can transform the energy, you cannot transform the events that produced it. *Second*, the witness is itself an octave of a field of consciousness which is highly subtle and non-egoic. It is non-dual and doesn't take sides. We will go into this in more depth later, for now practice not getting captured by the energy you are witnessing but feel as precisely as you can its *texture*.

Once you have experienced the quality and texture of the energy that arises, you will see its essence.

In a sense, that is the practice, the rest should flow from there. When you *see* something—see its nature and essence—you have contact with an irreducible truth and that stimulates *a knowledge event*. Knowledge informs, and unless you have some other aspect of you that is compromised, you act on that knowledge. Based on your knowledge you do not confuse, pardon the analogy, dog poop and chocolate mousse. One needs to be cleared away, the other is to be tasted. The witness is the bearer of knowledge.

The same is true internally, once you recognize that your *relationship* to some energy has made it toxic, you are in possession of knowledge and have actually begun to transcend the power of that energy to hook you. By *seeing* that you are carrying *Grade A Humiliation Energy* rather than being trapped inside the feeling of humiliation, you have already begun to process it. Instead of walking around as a humiliated person you become a person who *knows* what it is like to have been humiliated. Big difference! A person who is carrying *Grade A Humiliation Energy* will, one way or the other, start to show signs of negative stress in their behavior or their health or both. The person who has transformed the energy, because they recognized its toxic nature, but who knows clearly what it is like to be humiliated, is more likely to use that knowledge to avoid humiliating others. In the first case, transference of the stress in some form is likely, in the second, we are likely to see social benefit and the expression of higher values. Out of knowledge comes discernment and wisdom. *May you grow in knowledge!*

May you carry the knowledge of wounding so that you might heal others rather than transferring your wounds on to others out of ignorance. May you witness so deeply the affliction of hurt and betrayal that you always take that energy when it arises and free it of the pain of self-torment. May you be the torch of the true positive that exists in the core of all being. Though you find yourself taken to places of testing may you rise from those times—greater, stronger and wiser. May the witness within lead you to your own beauty in the heart of the mystery.

The Witness in Action: Death Row and the Killing Fields

Here is a story of two people asked *to bear witness* to human suffering and demonstrate humanity's ability to reach for higher ground:

I am standing at the door to the Marriott hotel in Washington and there is a long pause, for at that moment Arn Chorn Pond asks Marie Deans a question filled with the pain of one who survived genocide while so many others were taken. *"Why me, Marie?"* Again a pause, *"Because, Arn, you and I are called to be sacred witnesses."*

I had, as the Washington Office Director of *Amnesty International*, invited Arn and Marie to speak at a Human Rights Day event. Marie had responded to the tragic and brutal murder of her mother-in-law by publicly asking that the person responsible not be executed. Marie became deeply committed to trying to end this form of public violence and even accompanied men on death row and in their last hours before execution. Despite the horrific stress of this work she continued, execution after execution, to offer soulful and compassionate accompaniment to men facing the ultimate punishment. Arn was a very young boy when he was picked up, flute in hand, by the Khmer Rouge. That day, other children who were taken to the temple area where they were held, had their heads smashed against the wall. Arn survived because someone capriciously decided that he could play the flute for the soldiers. He became the flute player at genocide. He saw so much atrocity and carnage it can never be erased from his memory. Finally he escaped to Thailand through the killing fields and was adopted by Peter Pond, an American. *"I know that I am alive today,"* he told the Washington audience, *"not because bullets failed to kill me; I am alive because I have learned to love again."*

Arn and Marie are luminous human beings: they chose to take unbearable experience and be witnesses—by this I mean that they can tell us truthfully of the horrors created by humanity's lowest impulses and, at the same time, speak from a higher center; one which calls us to compassion, and to a love so powerful it lifts us all to a place where we experience what is truly means for human souls to evolve.

I wonder in a world undergoing such intense challenge and suffering, where are *you* a witness? There is work to do both on the inside and the outside: negative stress at the personal level and at the collective level. The only way we can look back at our own lives, or at our collective history, and really take hope, is if we transform negative stress as a path to something higher for ourselves *and* for the generations to come.

Indeed, as we shall explore later, negative stress can have its positive value, if it helps us grow in knowledge. Just as you cannot know love unless you have somehow communicated with love and been in its presence, so perhaps, if you have experienced hurt and then gone one step further to witness what hurt has done to you, you have the most defining existential choice: *'Will I finally transcend my own hurt so as to be* able *to ease the hurt of others?'* You cannot do the latter easily if you are still permitting old hurts to hurt *you*, if they are churning inside you and coming into your psyche *as waves of unresolved stress.* I am not claiming that what I have called the knowledge event, using the non-judgmental witness, is the only balm for inner hurt and wounds, but it is one that must be applied at some point if we are going to gain higher knowledge.

We have explored just how willing you are to go the distance to find your authentic self and that has led us to examine the subtle plane with regard to trapped energy and transforming negative stress, let's now explore how to tune into and harness positive energy for the same creative purposes. If you can learn to shake hands with that old stuff that has haunted you for so long—*"Hello darkness my old friend you have come to visit me again"*—can you also learn to bathe in the inextinguishable light of your own multifaceted, gorgeous and irrepressible being? Can you not only find, but live inside, the deep true positive at the core of your own being?

5

Engaging Subtle
and Elusive Positive Energy

"May the beauty of what you love,
be the work that you do." — Rumi

As we transform energy-drains and sink-holes, we have greater energy for creative engagement in the world. That energy not only lifts us up, if we are attentive to it and cultivate it, it invites us to stretch and grow. It points to new horizons. However, too often, we can find ourselves happy that we reached an even plateau, smooth going, and an accommodation with a secure dullness that tends to dim our capacity to tune into *more* creative energy—maybe because we know that if we look for it and engage it, it will lead to further challenge, or maybe because we are misers when it comes to living with abundant possibilities.

Once, when I had gone to spend a month at the Tibetan library and center in Dharamsala, I found myself laboring a little up the steep Himalayan foothills to the village of Mc Cleod Gang, when I was joined by a young monk. I asked him if it was a challenge to climb up and down the mountainside each day. It seemed like a lot of extra effort to get from A to B. "*Oh no,*" he exclaimed. "*I spent one month in New York City and my whole body—and soul—ached for something other than level ground. When I climb the mountain, I live the mountain and I breathe the mountain. The flat street does not give me that.*"

Perhaps, if we tuned in more often to the subtle promptings of a universe designed to offer us incredible expansion and growth, we would see that it is harder, and ultimately more stressful, to live in the comfort of the flat plateau than it is to face our next mountain.

In dealing with complex, demanding lives that are too full, we find ourselves wanting to get time off, put on the brakes and de-stress. But it seems to be a vicious cycle because our plateau of comforts is a fairly high maintenance place to be. We work harder in order to have the things, and the opportunities, to go places that will ease it up a bit for us. The acceleration of life is numbing. The theologian Thomas Merton viewed the constant busyness of modernity as a form of *violence* and a hundred years before him, Oscar Wilde had quipped, "*We live in an age when people are so busy they have become stupid.*" Given the fact that we have upped the pace considerably since then, I wonder if that makes us '*dumb and dumber.*'

Now you will hear from both medical experts and spiritual teachers that you must relax, give up the frenzy and that you can't achieve much anyway if you are frazzled. Since you are grown up, I am going to assume that you have received that message by now. I have made it clear this book is not about teaching you relaxation techniques, that would be entirely redundant. But I wish to remind you that relaxation and blobbing, or switching off, are not the same thing. Relaxation is often derived from strenuous activity or really focused concentration. Playing 18 holes of golf can be tiring but profoundly relaxing; spending an hour on the crossword puzzle can so much take your mind off the worries of the day that it leaves you deeply relaxed. This in itself is a clue to creative stress.

Where I want to lead you is to really embrace creative stress as your vehicle for personal transformation. To do that you will need to spend a little more time attuning to your own interior energy grid and learn to respond to the subtle call of *positive energy*—specifically learning to catch those elusive butterflies of your own intuitive faculties, those high frequency signals from your conscience and evolving consciousness, and those subtle promptings of your higher mind and soul. What I cannot guarantee is that they will be stress free. Nor can I claim that it is so easy to find, "the beauty that you love," as Rumi put it. We have to be able to recognize and appreciate beauty before it can reveal its fullness and depth to us. You will find, if you take Beauty as your teacher, it will teach how to recognize the value of everything, Beauty has a store-house of positive energy. Let yourself be aroused by the beauty of something and you will feel an in-flow of positive thoughts and feelings. Make everything you do a contemplation of beauty and you become an advanced mystic! But, for the moment, let's see if in our own internal energy grid we can cultivate more positive and dissolve more negative.

This may be a simple equation but let's see if it works: negative energy pulls energy in order to drain off more energy, like the idea of the insatiable *Hungry Ghost*. Positive energy pulls energy in order to create more energy, like fruitfulness, satiety or abundance. This is entirely simplistic at one level. In the next section of the book we will examine a non-dualist framework, and even have a different relationship to positive and negative but our mastery, for the moment, requires that we harvest positive energy and recognize where negative energy is the rodent who sneaks in at night to steal our grain.

Where are the places your soul experiences lift—that primal energy which carries the emotions upwards; that excites your curiosity; that awakens your sense of connectivity and flow; that stirs your passion for ideas or for social justice; that offers you love in its myriad forms; that invites you to laughter and to play and where you are touched by beauty?

Where are these positive forces in your life and how are you cultivating them? If it is music, how are you cultivating time and space for music? If it is social justice, how are you getting involved? If it is Nature, how are you spending time, quality time, in the natural world? If it is meditation, what is your daily practice? If you are not even completing your basic homework in this regard, forget about more subtle attunement. If this is an issue for you, I suggest you take a little inventory of what nourishes your heart and soul and then look at how you are cultivating those things in your life.

So let's assume you have done so and are genuinely looking at cultivating a higher attunement, how do you make progress?

First, be assured as fast as your ego mind zoomed past the closets with stored and unresolved stress, it goes as fast by any doors which smack of real positive growth. After all, from its perspective, that's just a different form of stress. We need the witness as much to see positive as negative. Remember when I use the word *positive* here I am not talking about *false positive*. *False positive is negative in disguise.* I am talking about positive, beneficial energy that is based in truth, integrity and which is free, fecund and healthy.

Positive energy has a signature sweetness in the body, just as negative energy has its own distinct biochemical array, so does positive energy. When we place in our hearts someone we are close to and shower them with feelings of love, our heart creates a veritable symphony of pleasure expressing hormones, endorphins and DHEA. When we are doing the things we love these 'molecules of emotion' increase our sense of well-being and gift us with more fluid attention. Compare the brain of someone negatively stressed and someone immersed in feelings of compassionate engagement and one will look 'all over the place' and, like computer files which need to be 'de-fragged.' The other will be more synchronized and orderly. In fact, scientific research shows if you are in sustained loving relationships, or if you are altruistic, you will live a longer and healthier life. If you haven't forgiven someone and you bring up your connection to them, you will, more likely than not, experience cardiovascular constriction, in other words your own body has its way of saying, '*Release it, let it go. Holding the negative stress of a grudge, or more serious resentment, is only going to hurt* you.'

Since the body mirrors our inner states in different ways, it will be good at this point to recall *how your body responds to different positive energies*:

- *that subtle shift in your breath when you are listening to your favorite music*

- *that delightful expectancy forming as a smile when your favorite person is on the way to see you*

- *that swarming sensation in your solar plexus when you have decided to go ahead with an important initiative*

- *that heart glow when you make up with someone after a tiff*

- *that feeling of boundless possibilities when your brain is teeming with bright ideas*

- *that warm glow that radiates throughout your body when you are sensually aroused*

- *that feeling in your gut when you sense some good news is coming your way*

- *that luminous quality of vision and connection with a larger reality when your heart and mind seem to perfectly synchronize*

- *that flush of strength and satisfaction that you feel as your muscles relax after a workout or a hike*

And in case you don't want to stop, keep adding on your own list!

Then keep going with a recall of *when and how* you have your most positive feelings:

- *you are recognized and appreciated for hard work, for excellent ideas, for amazing cooking, for clever problem-solving*

- *you feel accomplishment for what you have achieved, for outstanding effort, for things invisible to others but of value to you*

- *you are expressing love, making love, being loved*

- *you feel peace, oneness with others*

- *you are volunteering, working to improve social justice, nurturing others*

- *feeling safe and snug and reading a great book or watching a great movie*

- *your mind is being expanded*

- *you witness momentous changes on the political landscape*

- *your hidden qualities are brought out*

- *you have supported or been supported by a friend*

- *you feel the glow of solidarity with others or in spiritual community*

- *you feel grateful and blessed for one thing, or many things, or everything, when you feel deep spontaneous laughter*

- *you feel completely accepted for who you are—by yourself or others*

We could go on, and as with the *somatic* list, please do, if you are inspired. Make sure you are recalling the *feeling* of the experience.

There is much literature on developing positive, life-affirming energy. There are meditative, yogic and chi practices which, if you persist with them, will help you build up your reserves of positive energy. If too often you find you are depleted, and hanging on by the thread of sincerity or last minute prayer, learn a practice that will give you a head start when the really difficult stuff comes your way.

Now one more list, please.

This list is about the positive energy that arises *in adversity, challenge and testing:*

- *when you rise to a challenge that was truly daunting*

- *when you surprise yourself at your inner strength and resources during a difficult time*

- *when you live through a noble commitment despite personal sacrifice*

- *when you respond to an inner call that will test you greatly*

- *when you listen to your conscience even though it is inconvenient*

- *when you throw yourself into the accomplishment of your dream despite lack of resources or the skepticism of people who matter*

- *when you face down judgmental criticism because you believe in what you are doing*

- *when you come through the dark night of the soul*

- *when you stand up for truth amidst hostility or hypocrisy*

- *when someone calls you out and you are grateful*

- *when you get up for the hundredth time after you have fallen down*

- *when you face what you had been hiding from*

- *when you muster the courage and strength to kick a bad habit or an addiction*

- *when you finally bury the hatchet*

And the list goes on! And in case you are not familiar with the law of attraction—bless, affirm, and celebrate the positive and you will find yourself swimming in more positives than you had thought possible.

But true positives must be cultivated! Sometimes the positive hangs back, waits in the wings, has to wake from a trance—has to be summoned. Sometimes it only comes when you are ready to hear the still, small voice within or follow the wisp of an intuition. Yes, luring the positive out of hiding takes as much practice as unraveling the knots of negative stress.

The question is do you really want to go all the way, to be who it is your soul is calling you to be? In *the handshake* we suggested that you get to a place where you decide to go as far as you can in activating your inner core, and that your relationship to stress is now different—you cautiously welcome it because you realize that once you learn to really engage it, it carries you ever more deeply into your life's purpose. You have begun to learn how to transform negative stress, into higher creativity. We concluded that this required dismantling of the fortress of the conditioned mind and taking on the greatest adventure possible for a human being which is the fullest possible illumination of your spirit. Let's apply *a stress test* to see where you are, shall we?

Stress Test: Flatland, Bogland, or Higher Elevation

You have become more attuned to your own inner energy grid, and how your psyche deals with positive and negative charge.

So how are you doing?

Flatland

'Fine,' you say. What you mean is that there are highs and lows and you are modulating them, or to be more honest, seriously controlling them. You don't want it very high for too long because you fear you might have to face a come down or heavy disappointment, which is a stress avoidance strategy. You don't have the energy to deal with the stuff that you have pushed down, or shelved, for fear that it will weight you down too much and you won't have enough energy to climb out of the hole, which is a stress avoidance strategy. You are essentially living a soul numbing or even a soul destroying compromise. Your creativity is limited. It is more mechanical, less unique, more predictable. In a way that you may fail to recognize, you are cheating on yourself, your true self.

Bogland

'Great,' you say. But you know that is a lie. *'Lousy,'* you say, well that is honest at least. Whether you are in denial or you just can't hide it, you find yourself constantly trying to avoid feelings which drag you down or burden your conscience. This requires a lot of energy and you are like a person who is always having to take a long and circuitous journey to get somewhere. This means you are almost never at home, in the true self. Sometimes when it is really bad, you find yourself not going around them, but falling into one bog after another. You are very stressed, whether it is yet obvious to others or not. Your creativity is

blocked and this may push you into extravagant efforts to make it seem that you are on top of your game, or finally, to begin to recognize your stress and reach out for help.

Higher Elevation

'*Really good, thanks.*' You may or may not have a lot happening in your life, but the quality of attention you give to whatever you do—at work, at rest or at play—ensures deeply authentic engagement. You are present. You are also increasing your capacities, particularly the ones that need development, whether it is patience, courage, good humor, concentration, team playing, or compassion. Whether people see it or not, your life is intense and always filled with opportunities for real growth. You are moving from restlessness to peace without compromising freshness and audacity in engaging your responsibilities to yourself and others. As you climb upwards your vision and your more panoramic perspective on life grows: you gain an attitude of reverence for whatever sheer cliffs suddenly appear out of nowhere and which force you to invent new ways to proceed. Whatever unfolds in scale of difficulty or challenge you find yourself increasingly able to be grateful for the adventure and thankful for the way you are brought closer, and closer to your home in the true self.

When it comes to life, no categories of experience are as tight and clear as the metaphors or symbols we create to represent them. Life cannot fall into neat and tidy formulas. So whether you feel that flatland, bog, or higher elevation work as a concept for you, or that you are some hybrid of all three, I am simply going to ask you what are you doing with, "*this one precious life*" you have been given? *How have you really committed to your growth and maturity? How are you waking up?* Go into these questions and do not flinch. Give yourself a stress test!

You live at one of the most pivotal times in human history and these are decidedly complex, and fast-paced, times when we are witnessing both the promise and the peril of globalizing forces and conditions. We live in an age of spin, sophomoric media punditry, distraction and materialist fixation while Earth faces her greatest challenges. As Duane Elgin has pointed out, we reflect an adolescent phase of our development as a species: we have been trying on all kinds of techno-materialist thrills as we also try to find ourselves, and discover what we are about and what we really value.

When we are impulse driven, we are not taking the path to higher elevation, we are more likely as not experimenting at a lower level.

Ask yourself if you are doing all in your power to find higher ground— for yourself, your family, your community and the world.

Ask yourself if you are really willing to lead an ecstatic life.

Ask yourself if you really want to evolve beyond a plodding existence.

Ask yourself if you really want to climb the mountain of deep inspiration.

The climb begins when we first get a deeper inkling of the value of our own life and call to higher source for guidance. When we do so, we can easily provoke a counter-force, like the babble of the mind that gets stirred when we first try to meditate. We find we are disappointed that instant effort doesn't provide instant results. Then, with a little more effort, we experience a momentary high or some other makeshift response that may try to camouflage itself as the real McCoy. It's as if we first provoke a trickster element in the universe which lets us fall for the sham, the façade, to see if we really can tell the fake from the real or the surface from the depth. This is what I mean by immaturity; we can find ourselves *putting on the glitter and missing the gold.*

To fully enter into the promise of our personal and collective destiny we must learn not only to distinguish shimmer from substance but we must *become* what it is we truly value. At any given moment our lives are a reflection of what we value most, as much as we might profess certain values, if they don't reflect in our behavior—if they are not vividly incarnated—then we remain caught in our own immaturity. Life will do its best, it will conspire in endless ways, to move us into that mature place where we no longer simply long for, mimic or vaguely aspire towards the expression of our deepest ideals, but we become them. Life activates those stressful conditions not to make us suffer but to help us see that rather than flatland and bog, we are *destined* for higher ground.

If we are sincere we will get pushed over the edge of our own resistances or artificial sense of boundaries and limits. The progression from immature to mature is marked by initiations which serve to teach us about what is real, substantial and valuable. Initiations worthy of their name will scare off the ephemeral and take you to your true beginning, which is nothing less than the place where you make mature and binding commitments. If you are destined to go far, your initiations may even take the form of deep wounding and leave some scars. When we resist the bridge from immature to mature which initiations provide, we get stuck in denial and build a pretense, even an aggressive pretense, that ours is the desired lifestyle or the preferred creed. You may remember from growing up that one of the hallmarks of immaturity is obsession with being right, or at least being seen to be right. Being stuck in righteousness is the epitome of stress avoidant fear: the cohort of righteousness is fundamentalism, which is none other than an impenetrable flatland fortress surrounded by bogs and swamps.

The irony is that we can also miss the true gold of maturity and can go deeper into the glitter by piling one success on top of another, by building power and status, by learning to circumnavigate emotional complexities and suppressed feelings and by learning to live in a compartmentalized psyche. We need co-dependents to sustain our immaturity and there are always enough people willing to be co-opted into making things look good instead of allowing them to be real. It has become a social ritual to persuade each other that we are happy with *the symbols of success* rather than with happiness itself. It is a way of creating collective false positives in order to relieve our collective stress.

Developed societies have told themselves that the loss of community, and the sacrifice of simpler contentment for constant acquisitive up-grading is worth it, despite the fact that this attitude brings with it corrosive stress and a kind of servile relationship to stuff. We know in our hearts that the old cosmology, dependent on a God who gives an eternal reward to the good guys and a Hell forevermore for the bad guys, no longer seems so convincing. But we have not found a new story that can integrate spirituality with our current scientific and materialist understanding of the nature of reality, and so we play theme-park Earth for all its worth, and maybe to the last ride.

We have collectively gone so deeply into the glitter that we see on a global scale the success of spin over truth, marketing over meaning, and seduction over beauty. No one can predict or prophecy what will awaken humanity from its escalating materialist fixations to a full awareness of what is being lost. As scenarios for catastrophic systemic collapse and ecological devastation accompanied with the rise of war, crime and terror become more real, we have begun to see ever more clearly what is at stake. We are reaching an inevitable denouement when the gap between the values we profess and the values which we actually live by have become so great that no political spin and no religiosity can hide the chasm that grows with ever more tragic consequences.

The good news is that we can evolve beyond the level of consciousness that has precipitated our current crises: in fact there is evidence that a great transformation is already under way. But it is not a transformation that gets done to you, it is one in which you yourself participate emotionally, psychologically and spiritually. To experience a transformation of your own awareness from an unconscious alignment with regressive materialism, or one oriented towards thrills, fads and fashions to a more evolved, relationship-centered approach to life which is guided by conscious altruism and a conscience that is large enough to represent all-life—to experience such a huge shift requires that you become a mirror of your values. To move from being a verbal representation of your values to embodying them is essentially a spiritual process. It is one that requires you engage stress with a new understanding of what is at stake personally and collectively if you don't. There are no short-cuts, and the great spiritual masters of all times have made that clear. They say you must shed the distractions of immaturity and supplant them with mature commitment; you must die to be re-born.

Once we realize that we cannot duck the very force which will lift us, unless we want to go nowhere, then we change our stance from resistance to cooperation. When we let it carry us, it will invariably not be to Disneyland we go, but into a place where we are invited to live our values more deeply; a place where we will be offered an opportunity to leave our less mature selves behind us. It will be a place where we will gain the all-important fresh perspective of higher ground and that means bringing your higher, and more evolved self into the world. For *you are the mountain you climb towards*: inside you, there in the lofty ascent of your own being, and the creativity it gives birth to, the world will be re-created.

6

Revealing a New Perspective on the Truth About YOU

Not long ago neuroscientists discovered what they have come to call *mirror neurons*. It seems that these neurons fire in our brains as a kind of mirror of what is seen and experienced in the world. Imagine those neurons firing as you watch a game of tennis: your neurons fire as if you were in the game. They give you an interior experience of being in the other person's shoes. The conclusion that is drawn from observing mirror neurons is that more than just keeping score we are watching the whole narrative unfold. In the sports game you project what it must feel like to be winning or losing; you are evaluating the evidence for a change in the game, watching for outside chances, assessing the inevitable. You live the story as one of triumph or loss.

You don't just engage mirror neurons for sports, they fire constantly to give you a mirror of the narrative that is unfolding in any given setting or interaction with others. The neuroscientists suggest that the firing of mirror neurons is an essential component of empathy, because through them you are able to see the other as you, through the mirror of the reflection of other as self. They discovered that one of the issues for autistic people is that those mirror neurons do not fire and they live without a guiding sense of the narratives that are unfolding around them.

These findings underscore the significance of story in our lives: it is fundamental and constant. Coming in and out of our conscious minds, as the warp and weave of what we see as real, is the story we tell ourselves about our lives. So the very templates and structures of story which we hold inside us as our primary frameworks of meaning are critical to examine closely. They will reveal faster than you think where you have learned to greet stress as your teacher, where you have broken through resistances to give voice and shape to your own creativity and where you have repeatedly avoided meeting your greatest teacher. Look into your own story with that power of witnessing consciousness we have discussed and what you need to move forward will inevitably be revealed.

Let's look at some life-story scenarios. What is the meta-story—the overarching story—of your life that you tell yourself?

Is it a story of triumph against all odds? Is it a fame and glory story?

Is it a magical story? Is it a bad luck story?   Is it the luckiest person story?

Is it a side-splittingly funny story?   Is it a great mystery story?

Is it a holy story? *Is it a rebel's story?*   Is it a 'one day at a time' story?

Is it *'the big lie'* story?   Is it the 'I don't know' story?

Is it the 'I found salvation' story?

Is it the 'pull up a chair and let me tell you the story of my life' story?

Is it the *'if only'* story?   *Is it a love story?*   Is it a family story?

Is it a story of adventure and discovery?

Is it a story of wounding and healing?

Is it a story about great self-expression?

Is it a story about heroic or compassionate care of others?

Is it a story about leadership?   *Is it a story about recovery from abuse?*

Is it a redemption story?

Is it a story of never let the bastards grind you down?

Is it a savior story?   Is it a sly dog story?   Is it an addiction story?

Is it a success story? Is it a story of loss?   *Is it a story of miracles and blessings?*

Is it a story about lack of fulfillment?   Is it a story about vindication?

Is it a sexual liberation story?   *Is it a story about self- actualization?*

Is it a survival story? Is it a happy story?   Is it a sad story?

Is it a dull story?   Is it a story of deep betrayal?

Is it *'one hell of a party'* story?

Is it a transformation story?   Is it an enlightenment story?

Is it a *'how I'*, or a *'how we'* or a *'how they'* story?   Is it a Nature story?

Is it a plant medicine story?   Is it an E.T. story?   Is it a mystical path story?

Is it a story of power and influence?   Is it a story about money?

Is it a story about overcoming shame?   *Is it a story about punishment?*

Is it a childhood story?   Is it the unleashing of creativity story?

Is it a mythic story?   Is it a truth and justice story?

Yes, you have guessed it: the stories are endless and there is always more than one going on in a lifetime.

Why don't you re-read the list above and *choose the four stories that come closest to being the best amalgamation of your story.* Or if you like, take the list and do this with one other person or with a small group. Tell your story from a holistic perspective: the good, the bad, the ugly and the beautiful. Tell your story from the perspective of stress encountered as a teacher and/or the consequences of stress avoided. Telling the full truth about yourself—inside out—is probably one of the hardest things in the world to do. But try to be as honest as possible. And if you can't be completely honest with others, can you be so with yourself?

Guaranteed with this exercise the things that you don't bring up with others, or things that you even find difficult looking at in yourself, is where there is a swamp of negative stress stored up. Equally, you may hide from yourself and others your really big hopes and destiny dreams or your fear of disappointment. Maybe there is a deep aliveness in you that took the form of a vision or a calling that has been pushed back; a vivid and charged energy which gradually you fed to disappointment or numbness. *There is an existential stress that builds beneath the surface of so many lives—yet all that blocked energy can find its way to creative transformation.* This does not mean that the sugar plum fairy comes to make all your dreams come true. It means that we can experience a shift in consciousness that bathes us in an experience of a *reality which turns out to be more luminous and healing than any of our wildest dreams.* The dreams or the longings of our life change *form* and enter through the heart with greater simplicity and elegance than our more unfettered imagining. Yet the imagination, however unformed, is a vital part of the process; it is causal and primary because it moves us towards *the fire of incarnation.* Giving permission to that imaginative intensity about the story of your life—its meaning and purpose—is essential for this alchemical process of transforming stuck, blocked energy, in the form of negative stress and liberating its primal creative exuberance. If we tamp down our dreams, they will arrive unformed and confused into our lives.

Here, then, is the emergence of the spiritually maturing person, the one who has moved from *tentative handshake* with stress to a firmer and more resolute conviction that the *universe is to be deeply trusted.*

For the one who feeds the imagination and then surrenders to how it finds expression in the manifest realm of existence has opened up to align with primary source energy in creation. It should be clear by now that this energy seems often too bold, too direct and shocking. We tell it we are not prepared or able to deal with it, and so it coagulates into negative stress. But when we change our stance from defensiveness or intimidation, to a stance of trust and greater knowing—despite pain, shock, and difficulty—we realize that we are actually being guided towards fulfillment and grace. Keep going in that direction and, *"Everywhere you turn, there will be the face of God."*

Look deeply into the story of your life, no matter what it appears to be on the surface, it is a story of *becoming*. It is always a story unfolding. Don't let anyone ever tell you otherwise. You may have fallen way off the radar screen of your own admiration and respect and the good opinion of others. You may, in fact, have done things that were uncalled for and even despicable, but whatever the ruin experienced, there is no spiritual law I know of that does not in essence appreciate that energy, which has been taken into the darkest spiral of negativity, can be liberated, transformed and find its way to its natural, creative, life-giving power. Your story, whatever it is, always has outrageously positive potential.

Another way to look into the mirror of your own narrative, is to reflect on the archetypes, heroes and paragons of virtue that you are drawn to. When your back is to the wall, when you have been speared by tragedy, when you have fallen into a morass of despair or simply ache to realize your potential more fully, they are the mirrors of your true potential. The archetypes and heroes you choose will provide *templates for your own journey in transforming negative stress* and realizing your highest potential! The Handshake with stress is about transforming the stuck story into a heroic story of becoming.

Practice: Seeing Your Story in The Mirror of the Archetypes

We see ourselves in the mirror of others, especially in the lives of those who have influenced us most deeply, from our immediate circle to the heroes and archetypes we relate centrally to. Consciously or unconsciously we scrutinize how they meet and triumph over adversity. We assess their quality of being and stand in awe at the audacity and skillfulness with which they manifest their creative achievements. We live vicariously through them; we use them as models and templates of meaning. They inspire us and teach us how to bring essence out of its hiding place in the eternal realm of the soul and carry it across the threshold of every form of resistance into the everyday world of choice and decision. They are candles that burn bright in our darkest hour; the flame that no cross-current or stormy wind can extinguish. They represent the evidence that spirit comes to incarnate in flesh and blood reality. Those whom we are drawn to as way-showers help us sustain patience, tenacity, courage and compassion. Again, and again, through history we see that progress is achieved by people whose sustained communion with the life-force sources humanity's greatest generativity and creativity. As profoundly stressful as their lives can be, they are not de-railed by negative stress, instead their testing reveals the quality of their character and the nature of their gifts. It is worth summoning the stories of the great exemplars of creative stress, whether they are artists, poets, preachers, politicians or social reformers.

By meditating on their lives, and their struggles, they prompt us to cross the threshold of our own fears, inhibitions and perceived limitations. Most importantly they catalyze our own higher imagination—a substance so vital that it cannot be underestimated. In fact, Albert Einstein, one of the truly great creative geniuses of the 20*th* century noted, "*Knowledge is limited, but what encircles our planet is imagination.*" Truly it is imagination which floods the little platform of the rational mind with waves of intuition and mysteriously charged feeling—inviting, nudging and prompting us to listen to a calling that comes from our own hidden heart of hearts. When our own story feels undernourished, or a little jaded, our imagination can ignite a new sense of possibilities and latent capacities. Perhaps, nothing stirs imagination as much as witnessing how others walk through the fire of intense challenge and gift us with their luminous wisdom, courage, originality and sheer vitality. And nothing feeds negative stress more than a story that feels as if it is going nowhere.

See if you can find a couple of people, or a small group, to explore with you what speaks to you directly about a transformational relationship to stress in the lives of five people you admire or who have influenced you deeply.

Here is how to set up the exercise: Choose five people: they can be living or dead; they can be famous or unknown, historical or even mythic. Choose them from different categories: one from your family circle, one from religion, one from the arts, from sports, from politics, from philosophy. You get the idea. There are many categories to choose from. Choose people whose creativity, originality, capacity to create beauty, heroism, audacity, vision, tenacity, pluck, ability to overcome severe odds, etc, inspires you and fires up your own desire to live more truthfully and brilliantly or to be more aligned with your passion and purpose in life. Now, before you begin sharing with the group, see what your choices may have in common and *why they relate in some way to your own story and your own relationship to stress, particularly in relation to the concept of creative stress.* You will see deep patterns in the lives you have chosen that are speaking to you, even perhaps, subliminally. Try to surface what is speaking to you about how negative stress was transformed through:

- *tenacity*
- *the power of forgiveness*
- *generosity*
- *spiritual charisma*
- *the ability to absorb hostility without returning aggression or getting stuck in wounded feelings*
- *speaking and embodying a truth that is not compromised by self-interest*
- *huge resourcefulness in expressing higher principles of love and compassion*
- *fearless activism that comes from spiritual vision and joy rather than pointing fingers at enemies*
- *embodying solutions rather than fixating on problems*
- *an ability to hold the flame of originality even in the face of cynicism and scorn*

Write a sentence about each and then a few sentences about what this means for you. It is important to do your own private work before engaging in a dialogue about creative stress with others.

The Greeks had a word for seed pattern and purpose: *entelechy.* Thus, the entelechy of an acorn is to become an oak tree. Dare to discover the loaded pattern in your own deepest story. What are the seed qualities that stir you to grow towards your highest self? One thing that seems true is that we never fully know what will show up until we are tested. So, by looking at our own seed stories and the stories of those who truly inspire us, you could say we are priming the pump for those times when the pattern of possibilities gets dilated into real world experiences. That is when we get to know who we are as beings destined to reveal spirit in the immanental fires of existence.

Let me share a story of a woman who was tested; whose greatness emerged out of the cauldron of fierce hatred. If you want to appreciate the true power of creative stress, let *her* life call *your* life out of hesitancy to incarnate your own hidden greatness. This story begins with an 'average' person walking to work.

A Woman who Lives with a Bullet Lodged Next to her Heart

First, her words: "On 17th August 1973, whilst walking to work with a colleague, who was a member of the reserve police force, gunmen opened fire. We were going into our building of work, we were civil servants.

I was shot with a sub-machine gun, was taken to hospital, 14 miles away, where I had emergency surgery. The bullet had entered through the top of my left arm, broke ribs, split my lung and lodged between my heart and main artery. Surgery lasted over 6 hours and I had to have 20 pints of blood. I was in Intensive Care Unit where my consultant told my family, 'I left her comfortable to die.' I spent seven weeks in hospital, then discharged and told to get on with my life."

You can imagine trying to pick up your life with a bullet literally lodged next to your heart. The sense of shock, trauma, grief and outrage must have been extremely intense. Nonetheless, Frances decided to face all those conflicting emotions and with some trepidation she decided to go to a retreat with *Towards Understanding and Healing*. One of the women who was heading this work who became a friend and mentor to Frances, was Maureen Hetherington—one of the great visionary activists for peace and reconciliation in Northern Ireland. Maureen, who is a friend and colleague, was pregnant when her husband

Douggie was brutally shot on his first day of work for the Ulster Constabulary. Douggie had to have his arm amputated as a result.

It was not easy for Frances but she opened herself to healing, knowing that the opening would not only stir her wounds but provide fresh challenges. This exemplifies the *handshake* with stress. Nowadays, Frances is engaged in continued efforts to promote dialogue between Protestants and Catholics. She transformed a catastrophically negative experience—a bullet which entered her body with the velocity of hatred—and instead of living a quiet life in private peace and security, she chooses to live in the challenging fires of sectarian peace-making. For her, the answer to her stress has been to nurture a more meaningful life, to summon up courage, to attempt to change the course of history, and to face down oppression and intolerance. When we were together in London Derry a while back, I was stunned by her quiet demeanour and humility. There with the evidence of another's fierce aggression and hatred lodged next to her heart, she still chooses to find her own highest self. Without such creativity and commitment—without such embodied virtue—where do you suppose humanity would be headed?

Let's tell each other the stories of those who become our greatest teachers and templates of higher consciousness. In their stories you will find that they not only shake the hand of stress, they dance with it.

7

Demonstrating the Capcities of Evolving Maturity

Here is what I know. There comes a point when you have truly begun to learn how to transform negative stress that you feel a more steady and dependable contact with your higher self. You are not easily triggered; you are deeply engaged in your own transformation and have a quality of empathy which others are drawn to; you have a new level of interpersonal fluency and social conscience that marks you as a deeply mature human being. You know that octaves of higher consciousness exist within you and you have begun to tap their insight and creativity in ways that bring them all the way through to your daily life. Up to this point you have experienced flashes of grace, moments of intense growth, times when your personal cup of awareness and presence has been filled and is even flowing over. You feel that you are experiencing the reward and the creative concentration of your life force, as a result of your willingness to live in deep integrity with every challenge you are given. These states offer you opportunities to know your true self and your own larger story. Then one day you find you have begun to *inhabit* that larger story.

You have also begun to witness that those fleeting states of grace have started to crystallize as new bedrock of awareness; as new ground of your being. It becomes impossible for you to live in denial or to play the old stress avoidant games of earlier years. You live a soul-motivated life and you have increased energy for meaningful engagement with those around you and with the world in general. You are someone who is more attuned to your own developmental curve and where others are in their growth. You are more sensitive to what is unfolding in your immediate environment as well as on the planet. And you have a fully ignited passion to go further: this means that you are not diffident or afraid when Life asks more of you. Rather than being on the treadmill of stress, desperate to find rest and relaxation, you are energized by anything which expands your vision, stimulates your higher imagination, and stirs your capacity for altruism. As unlikely as it may have sounded to you at an earlier phase of your development, you have found a source lake in the higher reaches of your own being, a reservoir of such depth and potential, that all you want to do is draw from it. Even when doing so means being prepared to be tested more, opened more, used more, and stretched more. Why?

Because now you know that creativity has its price and you are willing to pay an ever greater price to unleash its life-enhancing potential into a world imprisoned in the dense energies of materialist fixation, cheap thrills, quick-fix solutions; a world so hunkered down into the false polarity of frenzy and stress-reduction that it swings between hyper-acceleration and sedation; between induced excitements and numbness. But *you have found the great middle way* the mystics speak of where the heart is always alive and receptive to all that enters into its field. It doesn't need to seek the highs and avoid the lows because it trusts and knows that all that is needed is given, irrespective of the form it takes. When it comes with a heavier challenge, it is greeted not repulsed: *Hello darkness my old friend. You have come to visit me again.* When it comes as joy, it is honored and celebrated without cloying attachment. You can greet the darkness because now you know that it is not the end of the story.

The Sufis make a distinction between the *states* experienced in the process of becoming a mature human being and the consolidation of a *station* of development; what they refer to as the difference between *hal* and *makam*. What I am calling the handshake with stress leads to this station of the mature human being: it is a station which is marked by spontaneous creativity.

It is widely accepted in spiritual work, as in the work of becoming a more conscious human being, that we must let go of the rehearsed or conditioned mind: the part of us that knows the answer and knows how to respond because that was what it was taught or how it was brought into conformity. But there really is a place where we can respond from the originality and unrehearsed creativity of our own consciousness. To access spontaneous creativity obviously requires, not necessarily relaxation, but the absence of serious blockages of negative stress; those corrosive interference patterns that will inhibit anything that may arouse old wounds, trauma and aversions and anything that may demand that you live your true potential. It also requires what we have come to refer to as *presence—a place where one's consciousness is not distracted by mental noise, judgmental thinking and skittish emotions but where it is saturated in an open, empathic attentiveness.* Insight and healing spontaneously arise from the place where consciousness is clear and receptive. That seems so obvious, but getting there requires great integrity and commitment.

Mystics also agree that there is one more element that confirms this station: *longing.* Now by that they do not meaning pining or neurotic neediness. Longing emerges when you begin to sense that if you continue on the journey you will be pulled inexorably into the Source of your consciousness. You will merge into something which is unutterably great and completely free of fear, doubt and limiting attitudes and beliefs. You long for union with wholeness, with a harmony that integrates all the disconnected parts of your life and with a radiance which consumes you in unconditional love.

This longing will carry you through any fire because finally you know that the game is up, and that you are ready to surrender completely to what is given to you for your growth.

It is at this point you also realize with a kind of mystic thrill that the sheerest of mountains still lies ahead. There is a moment of respite, a time of deep awe and profound reverence before your Teacher invites you to embrace what appears to be an insurmountable difficulty. You meet what the *I Ching* refers to as *Mountain Arresting Progress*. And that, believe it or not, is a very positive and creative place to be. That is where you are going to embrace the mountain!

Before we go to the full embrace we have a little more work to do.

Maturing Humanity

We are evolving as a species; evolving in consciousness. Let's look at four indicators of the mature human being; four ways we transform negative stress to become creative instruments of higher consciousness:

Becoming a dialogic person

Becoming a subtle person

Becoming a healing person

Becoming a loving person

Becoming a Dialogic Person

You want to speak your truth coherently, after all it should be your best effort at representing who you are and what you believe. The more coherent you are, the more you will be able to communicate effectively, whether we are talking about intimate relationships, professional encounters or sharing your political, religious or philosophical beliefs with others. We cannot progress if we cannot share our truth with each other. But you do not want to be *hyper-coherent*: that is when every point you make is so exactly linked with every other point that there is a rigidity and inflexibility in what you are communicating. The truth likes to breathe; it is most true when it is most alive, not when it is dead certain. It comes alive when it is brought into relationship with other truth, when it is open and taking in new perspectives. Truth is illuminated by diverse perspectives and it is diminished by excluding fresh insights. Blocking other perspectives and fixating on absolute certainties is a marker of significant stress avoidance or repressed negative stress: what if you had to adjust your beliefs to incorporate hitherto unacceptable notions? What if you allowed yourself to radically change your beliefs? Depending on the context, this could put you in an embarrassing, difficult or even threatening situation; and so it would seem easier to hang onto the old certainties and avoid being exposed to ridicule and scorn, or even to being ostracized. There are understandable reasons why the truth stagnates: we are not willing to pay the price, and so we look for a cheap and easier version rather than face the demands it places upon us. I wonder how often the stress-avoidant ego invades conscience and struts around as moral superiority when in reality it is afraid to face a deeper truth.

Too often we define ourselves by the truths we hold, not by the way we hold them. But the way we hold them is pivotal at a personal and collective level. For if you can hold your truth in a way that provides a space for my truth to be heard, we will find that what is created is not only a greater truth but a more effective way to access truth. Nothing is more important for our maturation as a species than the emergence of true dialogue.

The critical next phase of our evolution demands that we learn how to honor both our unity and our diversity. The good news is that despite racism, ethnic hostilities, dominator models of development, and violent fundamentalism, the so called average person is becoming more tolerant, more inclusive and more skillful in multicultural and multi-ethnic environments. There is no doubt however, that there is need for massive educational initiatives to increase our collective capacity to engage in non-violent forms of dispute resolution, conduct genuine discourse about the core values that must become the basis of collective social practice whatever the nature of our theological or ideological disputes and to learn how to confront each other with awkward and inconvenient truths when necessary.

We cannot move forward if we are unwilling or unable to face the challenges and stresses that are inherent in dialoguing with difference. We must teach each other how to cross that threshold of difficulty and discomfort knowing that our greatest ingenuity, creativity and problem-solving abilities are stymied at our peril. We cannot be risk averse when it comes to the things that really matter. The neuroscientist Jerre Levy suggests that more than anything what seems to be the decisive element in how we humans develop is our ability to rise to challenge. Cross the line from the safe encampment of your point of view and enter the unknown with someone of a very different point of view and you are likely to be surprised by your own creative power. Remember dialogue is not about making false compromises to be nice to others. That's just more stress avoidance. It is more about reaching understanding and respect than it is about reaching agreement. As such, it is the basis for peaceful planetary civilization. And if I have an inkling about anything, it is that evolution has been engendering the emergence of the dialogic human, capacitated to live into the creative stress of transcending the unnecessary and often brutal ruptures triggered by our inability to dialogue about our differences.

Becoming a Subtle Person

Deepening dialogue and communication with others is, we know, much more than a verbal message sent, message received, message understood. Communication can be a complex weave of somatic, emotional, psychological, cognitive exchanges in highly contrasting contexts, environments and cultural settings. If we are striving to reach understanding, there can be confusing and conflicting elements to sort through, '*What he is saying sounds good, so why am I getting a bad feeling about this?*' Added to which we have uniquely individual and idiosyncratic ways of communicating ideas and feelings and cultural communication styles which are by no means universal. We are always picking up, consciously or unconsciously, different cues about the intention, character and deeper motivation of others as seen through our own unique filters and as reflected on the screen of our perceptions and awareness. Communication, and particularly dialogue, is not a blunt instrument.

Men, in general, are known to have work to do in this arena; and women are often decidedly superior in this regard. Much has been written about the evolutionary potential of the rise of the feminine and the promise it heralds of transforming dominator forms of communication. It is easy to block out signals we wish to ignore in order to force our point of view, to impose order, or control others, but all we do is delay the inevitable expression of feelings and perspectives that were bulldozed over. As consciousness evolves, it becomes more whole, more attuned, more able to read the soft clues of intuition and gut feelings, and sense what lies beneath the surface. It gives permission to intangibles where both unresolved issues may be hiding out and where reservoirs of potential remain untapped. Subtle communication understands that our transactions with each other have multifaceted dimensions and that as we hone our capacity to become aware of those dimensions we humanize the world around us.

The subtle person tunes into both their own and others submerged stress and, by being a witness to it, can acknowledge the hard stuff that needs to be dealt with. Contemporary society, where transactions with others often move at break neck speed, does brilliantly at ignoring anything but the superficially obvious. We have told ourselves that we don't have time to tune in to others, but where are we going if we don't? Our de-sensitization is our central problem and the way we have ravaged Nature is a mark of our grievous and bludgeoned numbness to the world around us.

Fortunately we live at a time when the big brash stories of success are obviously empty of meaning: all the get-rich-quick schemes and frenzy of corporate greed were built on the lie that we could tune out anything but limited self-interest. We live at a time when all of our clumsy learning as a species has brought us to a place where we have run out of shortcuts and the only way ahead is to delve deeper: to take the long road through the human heart and harvest its more profound creativity.

Becoming a Healing Person

The root of the word heal is to make whole. We have learned so much in the last thirty years about mind-body health and how our attitudes and beliefs have a significant role in our overall wellness. Peace of mind fosters health. Our inner lives are now the subject of greater scrutiny and it is very clear that unattended negative stress can do long-term damage. We have become aware of post traumatic stress disorder resulting from harrowing levels of stress. What we are less familiar with is what some psychologists have come to refer to as *post traumatic growth*. Even when catastrophic things happen to us we can draw tremendous insight and meaning from them and they can become catalysts for our growth.

I remind you of this because I do not think there is a linear trajectory to healing. Neat formulas for healing will not be found in this book, though I dare to hope that it will be healing in many other ways for those who work with its contents. Remember those who are terminally ill may experience profound emotional, psychological, and spiritual healing even as their bodies are dying.

Despite these advisories we have, in fact, learned a great deal about the healing power of forgiveness, self-acceptance, altruism, meditative practice, having positive attitudes, laughter, sustained intimate and loving relationships, having a passionate purpose and gratefulness.

Healing has been captured by the marketing gurus as so much about taking care of 'me'. We are invited to take spas, and supplements, and a host of other heath products that will help us recover from a stressful world. These things are all fine but the core of healing can never be in isolation, as if we could heal 'me' and not my relationship to others and to the world I live in. You cannot be whole as a separate entity, because you are not such a thing, nor has ever such a thing existed. You are interfused with the life of the one whose womb you emerged out of and immeasurably influenced by countless beings known and unknown. As you free yourself from all that prevents you from being more whole you will find how profoundly your liberation is tied to how you transform the relationship between self and others. Our wholeness is revealed in vast networks of interconnection and interdependence: a design that suggests we can only fully appreciate our diversity when we have discovered our unity. Modern society must re-discover the intimacy that indigenous cultures have strived at great cost not to lose. This is the intimacy of the realization that you and I live *inside* each other not *outside* each other. "*I am because you are.*" Ubuntu!

Becoming a healing person is to offer your most intimate sense of identification with your own wholeness and the wholeness of others and beyond just human to human, to other species and the web of life itself. Healers know wounding and suffering intimately—*and what human being does not?* What defines them is not whether they call themselves healers but how they use their experience to *extend themselves*. To be a healer one must cross the threshold of the ego into the uncertain territory where others may be triggered, hiding their wounds or hurting because they have never felt invited to be themselves. It is not necessarily a safe place to go, but when you venture far enough into it, no matter what rejection you experience, you will be overwhelmingly convinced that more than anything the world longs for healing.

Some years ago I had the privilege to participate in a conference in Bali: *The Quest for Global Healing*. The conference came as a response to the terrorist attacks. The Balinese leaders felt that the bombings were a clear indication that our world was in need of healing. It drew people from over a dozen countries and Archbishop Desmond Tutu, garlanded with flowers, gave the keynote address.

Tutu had presided over a commission in South Africa that represented a new vision of healing for humanity. It was guided by Truth, Reconciliation and Forgiveness rather than bloody vengeance and the continuance of racism and hatred. The proceedings of the commission are filled with evidence of the power of common folk to demonstrate the highest qualities of forgiveness and compassion. But they had one fundamental requirement that opened the way for grace to make its transforming entrance into this formal and official process as potently as it did: that requirement was truth. There, in Bali, Tutu reaffirmed the central role truth plays in laying the groundwork for healing the deep wounds inflicted in violent oppression. Wounds close over and live beneath the scar tissue of resentment; if unaddressed, they fester and poison the hearts of families and communities and are transmitted to the psyche of subsequent generations. The Archbishop reminded the conference attendees that if we are determined to heal a wound, *it must first be opened*. When we are able to stand in the presence of truth our wounds will open and *truth itself has the power to wash the wound*. Once *opened and washed* our wounds are *then* ready for a *soothing balm to be applied*.

We live at a time of artificial quick-fix solutions to our problems at the individual and collective level. We have been applying balm to closed wounds. It is time to end the pretense and, while we have time, to heal the thing we call modern civilization. That requires not grandiose pronouncements, and dazzling new healing remedies but work each one of us must do to reach out beyond our comfort zones, and sometimes our really comfortable comfort zones, and have the courage to touch the places where wounds crouch in hiding and brilliance waits to be recognized.

Becoming a Loving Person

Love is a form of deep generosity and deep receptivity; its amplified energy stirs movement and carries us in its flow. It tells us we are not stuck, that we are not prisoners, forever confined to the humdrum, to our perceived limitations or to past trauma. Love potentiates everything it comes into resonance with.

As the mystic Meher Baba once put it:

"Love and coercion can never go together; but while love cannot be forced upon anyone; it can be awakened through love itself. Those who do not have it catch it from those who have it. It goes on gathering power and spreading itself until eventually it transforms everyone it touches. Humanity will attain a new mode of being and life through the free and unhampered interplay of pure love from heart to heart."

Love crosses boundaries in the same way that healing does. It tells us that we are worthy. It tells us that we are never so busy, so pressured to succeed or to make ends meet that we cannot step into its warmth and trust. It takes the fragments of our lives and offers them waves of wholeness and connectivity. It says to the ever hungry sense of inadequacy that there is a place where our being can be fed and nourished just for who it is we are on the inside. It tells us that all the *accoutrements* of merit, success and achievement, or the lack of them, are never to be confused with our core. It plugs us into a reality that offers Life to whoever wants to live without a contract burdened by, '*if*' and, '*only under these conditions.*' Love says, '*dare to take me as I am*' not, '*as you would have me be.*' Love is a form of audacity that nudges you to free yourself from the energy of self-doubt—precisely because it is the only force in the universe that can enter into the self and cause it to remember its own irreducible beauty. Yes, Love can find your beauty under any circumstances. No matter what story you tell yourself in the fortress of negative stress and regret, it says: '*There you are in your essence.*' We are freed when we are truly seen and known. Freed from the *maya*, the illusion, that told us we could really only be ourselves under what turns out to be a very complicated, and contrived, set of conditions.

Please remind yourself that love is not necessarily nice, or tidy: it is an elemental force which blows through creation pushing one relentless question, "*Are you ready to be? Then come dance with me!*" Because it has this shocking capacity to honor the core of everything, when love is shared it ignites more love. As hard as it is to imagine humanity surrendering itself to this force as the next major phase of its evolutionary process, I say, "*Not really!*"—we are actually more than half way there.

From this perspective take another look at what stresses you out and how you might find a breakthrough response to that question, '*Are you ready to be?*' And if you just want to scream, '*Get real! I've got too much on my plate. I am stretched to the limit,*' ask yourself the question, '*If love nourishes us at the core, why am I so stressed?*' Maybe you could take time to explore the answer. Call a friend. Trust me, this one is worth the time.

Final Base Camp for Moving from the Handshake to Embracing Stress

What an achievement to have reached a place in your life where you appreciate that you can always keep growing as you create more meaning in your life. Scientists remind us that we produce dopamine in our brains when we experience a sense of reward—it is associated with pleasure and a feeling of high. But here's the kicker: if we are *anticipating* or *hungry* for reward and don't get it, we try to find it in another form—which is why we look for quick and easy surrogates after disappointment. We self medicate our rewards when life doesn't give them to us. The development of our more conscious and higher self requires that we learn how to identify more meaningful rewards. Human beings are meaning makers and the more we evolve, the more we expand our sense of what it means to live a meaningful life, the territory of meaning literally opens up to include vistas we had never imagined. We discover that our own being is expansive, and the more it is awakened, the more it is energized by noble qualities and ethical pursuits.

You have reached a place in your life where you now understand what a perverse distortion it is to miss out on *the sustained high* of one who has learned how to be generous, loving and forgiving to others, or one who has understood that altruism is a form of pleasure not easily matched by the most elaborate self-indulgence, simply because the initial cost seemed too great. We live in an age when it is easy to become junkies of instant rewards which are *bought* to entertain us, soothe us, or give us status. The quick fixes for negative stress get quicker and quicker but like fast food they tend to lack nutrition. They just don't ever access the profound sense of reward we experience when we challenge ourselves to stretch and live more meaningfully.

If you have truly advanced in transforming negative stress you will have left behind the *'great deal'* and *'unbelievable bargain'* shopper's approach to life. You will be in a place where you have consciously chosen to pay for what you value.

You will pay with courage and be rewarded with self-esteem. You will access your own moral imagination and it will prompt you to turn the world as you know it upside down:

- *when everything tells you that you have no time, you give time to something more meaningful*

- *when you are told to do the sensible and conformist thing, you choose instead to do the thing that expresses your heart's desire*

- *when you are told you might be smacked down for speaking up, you find your voice*

- *when everything but your gut tells you that taking a certain course of action is a dead-end, you listen to your gut*

- *when you realize that the numbness of living so many half-truths is greater than the pain you may endure in trying to live your truth, you willingly face the pain*

- *when you realize that you must change, even if no one else is ready for change, you dare to lead*

- *when you try to dance in the ashes of your own despair, and it doesn't work, you learn that walking is just as beautiful*

In this mature and evolved state, your life may not be radically different on the surface. You didn't need to spend time with gurus in the Himalayas and you didn't find the need to run around proselytizing the latest amazing way to accelerate everything from your material needs to finding the perfect mate, or speedily realizing your soul's purpose. There isn't necessarily much drama about your growth and development. But in a way that people notice, you are a safe harbor in the storm. You have a capacity to listen to them with your whole being; they learn to trust that rather than projecting your philosophy onto them, you draw from them what they need in any given moment. Your life has tones and

117

contrasts as it finds its own music. You don't need to get rid of the drums or the brass, and you are not afraid to sound the flutes—*you have found your range.*

But none of this makes you complacent, because you know there is a climb ahead. You are energized by the possibilities of a more liberated life. You have not shed fear completely but you have enough centered peace in your heart that, when it comes, you ask it reflective questions and find yourself opening to answers that take you to the root of issues that are yours to work on in this lifetime. Rather than being jaded by your stuff, you know there is no more productive place to put your energy and apply all that you have learned on the journey. This is the beginning of true serenity.

What I am calling the base camp for moving from the handshake to embracing stress is a place where your issues—the residual blockages of your life's experiences and how you have handled them—become clear. Your consciousness has become sufficiently uncluttered that they stand in bold relief. You know that if you are to progress, you can no longer ignore or go around them. In fact precisely because you decided to first have a truthful encounter with them and then to open fully to them, they are now front and center. What was once your nightmare is now your chosen work. You are beginning to release the extraordinary transformational potential of your own higher self, what I referred to earlier as your soul power. The witness, which you have learned to access as an octave of higher consciousness, is now firmly established and ready to help you see the essential qualities of that which still remains blocked and tangled in your psyche.

Let's remind ourselves that the witness is not a version of the inquisition: it is not there to judge and punish the guilty, to root out the bad eggs and prosecute the heretics. *It is the non-judgmental seat of enlightened compassion and awareness which reveals the true nature of things.* Once employed, the witness creates a knowledge process that identifies the nature of the distortion. In its own very precise way, it gives you a pitch perfect read on the octave or frequency of certain emotions or states of being.

If, for example, one of your knots is around a profound resentment at the way you were treated by someone, the witness will allow you to know what an unrefined energy resentment is, as clearly as a science teacher can demonstrate the nature and qualities of sulfuric acid. In reality one cannot love or hate sulfuric acid, one can only know what its qualities are and that it is best not poured over the skin. Similarly when one knows that fuelling resentment is akin to pouring sulfuric acid over your heart and mind, that knowledge guides us towards releasing the resentment. Once the knowledge is there, release practices of deep breathing, loving kindness and forgiveness will transform this corrosive and stressful energy—leaving you with one less issue to deal with!

You are now ready for a whole new order of growth. Rumi once said, "*Those who jump in the fire, end up in the water. Those who jump in the water, end up in the fire.*" The direct encounter with stress is all about learning how to jump in the fire: how to face your difficulties even when it seems as if you could side-step them and go sip martinis by the pool. The handshake is even more about living in the fire of deeper purification and burning off the stuff that holds you back. You do all this not because you are downbeat and a masochist, but because you know that when the fire has burned all the way through, nothing will hold you back from jumping into the current of that natural and ecstatic life-source which gives you the vitality to live the life you were given with abandonment to your own higher self. By now you have learned that when you engage stress it is not the negative and disruptive force you once thought, it is your greatest teacher and the source of tremendous growth and creativity.

You are now on the threshold of complete trust. You know irrevocably that your own consciousness emerged from a clear stream of reality, and that rather than being stranded in an alien world where conditions are anything but right for you to experience that source reality, you find that your arms are open wide to embrace it. It is so *deeply familiar*, so beloved, so completely the answer to your longing. Mystics speak of this deep soul recognition as a state of remembrance: the heart of the universe and your own heart are one.

But, as you are about to find out or remember, it is a reality, once embraced, which changes utterly what you once thought to be true. It is a reality which quickly informs you that your sincerity and commitment have only prepared you for an epic adventure. The path to your highest self is generally sequential up to this point and then it seems to end abruptly—as if once you have headed out of your high altitude base camp, you are confronted with what seems an impassable chasm. This experience can precipitate a spiritual crisis and an entirely unexpected visitation of stress where you least expect it. You finally open your arms in deep surrender and trust to the universe and the first thing you get in return is the edge of an abyss. *What's going on?* Just when you thought the embrace was going to be the cozy ending, it turns out to be the ultimate stress test. Let's explore the Mystery of your final liberation.

.demonstrating evolving maturity.

.level three.

the embrace

8

Embracing Paradox and Fully Incarnating Belief

You have to have a sense of humor. You were becoming so virtuous. You had made a great shift from getting upset and frazzled by stress triggers, to being able to handle almost anything with a fair degree of equanimity and aplomb. You had developed an authentic sense of reverence for Life as your teacher. You had grown so much; even noticed that you were recognized and appreciated by others for your steady hand in a crisis, your empathy for others and the quality of your insight into the human condition. But instead of being rewarded and carried even higher into the angelic realms you find yourself confronting an impassable chasm—a dead end.

What is going on? The linear progression of your development at some point gets halted: the language, the concepts and the basic worldview that were the ladder for your ascent towards the station of an evolved and mature human being eventually short-circuit. When confronted with the true nature of your higher self you can literally experience a deep existential crisis, and sometimes if you are heading in that direction, Life will give you an extra shove. It is as if you are given a message that you want to reject, informing you that the old rules do not apply. You are told, '*In order to proceed you will have to undergo deep transformation.*' To which you reply, '*And what do you think I have been doing?*' Those who know this place talk about experiencing betrayal, undergoing a harrowing loss or wounding, struggling with a sense of emptiness, a shattering of the personality—the dark night of the soul.

In the final initiation which leads to the full embrace, the wild energies of the universe blow at full strength. '*Now we will see what you have really learned,*' the universe seems to be saying, not malevolently but more like the loving doctor of the soul who wishes to make sure that you have healed enough to be able to fully enjoy the new life which lies ahead of you when you have recovered.

There is an aphorism: "*You possess only that which survives a complete shipwreck.*" Essentially, this final stage is about helping you see where you have stored baggage which will prevent you from progressing further—conceptual baggage, ego baggage, unresolved issues baggage. This is where cognitive dissonance come into the picture as we confront the reality that the things we hold onto are the very things which will pull us down, and the things we release will save us from drowning. Just when we thought we were developing an appreciation for the subtle, it seems to get way too subtle for our liking.

We like having a good reputation, being admired by others, gaining the respect of peers, feeling good about the job we are doing, getting the helper's high, making significant contributions to community life and social good. These are all part of the positives we feel we have developed by cultivating a healthy relationship to stress and which seem to be a welcome reward for living faithfully, passionately and courageously. But there is a worm in the apple of our good fortune: despite our best efforts, ego slips in and takes credit for every good thing that results from our efforts and assigns blame for the crud when things unravel. Ego resides in the dualistic framework. It is not bad, but it cannot cross the chasm that exists between duality and non-duality. On one side of the chasm it lives, on the other it is dissolved.

But ego does not explain everything. I, for one, cannot explain all that humans have to endure or resolve, all our pain and suffering, by laying it at the door of ego. Terrible things happen to good people: tragedy befalls them, successive forms of misfortune seem to beset some more than others, despite the evidence of their decency and lack of malevolence. I know that our attitudes and beliefs are deeply implicated in how we heap upon ourselves ruinous consequences and that transforming them can dissolve negative charge and accumulated stress. But even *then* we meet calamity in the form of hurricanes, toxic poisoning, violent assault, political domination and oppression and the myriad consequences of the immature, unskillful and exploitative behavior of others.

Much is made about the laws of attraction these days and the notion that if you are not having a perfect life, all you need to do is realize you have been attracting the wrong things and while, again, there is some truth in this, it just doesn't explain all. Are the victims of genocide, terrorist attacks, torture, rape, toxic dumping, or pandemic diseases individually responsible for attracting these misfortunes?

There have to be other frameworks of meaning that can provide perspective on this—*in order to be able to embrace ultimate stresses, each of us will need for our peace of mind to contemplate and live into the belief which most speaks to us.*

Belief acts as the foundation of meaning—it is essential for our development; and in a riveting new theory, Bruce Lipton suggests in *The Biology of Belief* that there is a deep correlation between belief and the activation or suppression of genes with positive or negative traits. It gives mind a map which we cannot now healthily live without, but please remember as you grow in knowledge it also becomes necessary to revise your beliefs.

Let belief be passionately held and radically open to transformation. Let it breathe. Let it burn its way through every compromise and accommodation which suggests that you do not have to live your belief with passion and purpose or that you do not have to be accountable for your beliefs because you can bob along in the crowd and no one will notice the dreary half-life of un-awakened belief that you allow yourself to live. To be able to *embrace* stress, your belief cannot be narrow or single pointed. When you really live inside your belief there will be space for others to awaken to their beliefs: you will be open, not closed.

Practice: Belief Statement

As an exercise, I recommend that you create your own belief statement and look at your life in relation to that belief. This is also a good excrcise to get together with others, share and dialogue about once they have also completed a core belief statement. Here are three templates to get you going, *but you must create your own:*

> *I believe* we evolve as a species into higher orders of development based on our learning in specific contexts; what held tight knit clans together has to be shed for collaboration in larger and larger contexts and all the way to the formation of global community. We constantly shed the old ways in favor of more inclusive, democratic systems which evolve towards universal human rights, justice for all, and the greatest protection from violence, and exploitation. In this map, we keep weaving inner growth and development with societal and global structures which are more ethical and reflect values

127

that ensure the most optimal survival of our species and earth habitat. My personal journey is about living and representing these higher social norms and values because we live in a time when it is necessary to transform the old systems or face unimaginable levels of breakdown and destruction. When I fail to achieve these ethical standards myself, when I fail to be an advocate of ecological values and social justice, I suffer, increase the suffering of others, and participate in the rapid environmental degradation we see all around us.

I believe that consciousness exists independently of human life and that it is the crucial element in drawing humanity towards higher truth about the nature of reality. This consciousness is essentially loving and nurturing and we evolve towards its qualities and capacities when we live loving and compassionate lives. This field of consciousness permeates all life and is causal—we become enlightened individually and collectively when we understand how consciousness functions and when we fully cooperate with its purpose and principles. When we die our consciousness survives and at some point reincarnates at the level it achieved in the prior incarnation. I believe the universe is filled with many levels of conscious life. When I encounter recurrent difficulties, they flow from my lack of consciousness, my inability to cultivate higher consciousness or from the karmic inheritance of previous lifetimes. I know that the planetary-wide shift in consciousness is possible and that I must do everything I can to help nurture this collective enlightenment.

I believe in a divinity who is all-powerful, and the creator of our universe. This divinity is beyond my knowing and is both personal and impersonal. God has sent prophets and messengers to humanity and incarnated in flesh to show me how to live and given rules and precepts which must be followed. Worship of God in His Infinite Mystery and Indivisibility is an absolute requirement to ascend to be with Him after the body dies. At which time there will be a reckoning or judgment of how faithfully I followed his commandments. I will suffer in this life and my soul will suffer in the hereafter if I am not faithful to the ways God has shown us. It is imperative that I do my part and that we work together, whatever our religious perspective, to represent and embody God's love and compassion for all beings.

There are countless other ways to configure and represent belief about life, death, spirit and eternal reality. I leave it to you to write a paragraph which encapsulates the essence of your own belief. Post it on your refrigerator or put it on your altar and let it be your compass or your way to check in with how vividly your life is a reflection of this belief. Then make sure to add to it or revise it from time to time. As you grow your belief will expand and grow.

But be clear about this: *your ego will truly run amuck in the absence of a coherent belief structure.* It will make it up and then change it with ease. It will follow the latest trends and then ditch them when they are exposed or ridiculed. The ego loves coasting, because that is how it protects you from feeling the pinch of stress when Life asks you to represent your core beliefs and values: '*No need to sweat the hard stuff,*' it says, '*Make it easy on yourself. Right?*'

Belief has a bad rap, as if it is always rigid and inflexible. Think of it as something alive and in movement, like the homing device that carries birds across continents taking them to their nesting places and feeding grounds. It is your inner guidance system which tells you whether you are flowing towards Reality or away from it. It has to be able to course correct in the face of new evidence. There is a quality to the believing heart which always remains open and which offers itself as willing. "*Teach me,*" it says, not as a child afraid to make a mistake, but as one whose growth has been marked with awe and reverence for an ever-expanding journey.

And when that journey has taken you to the moment when you face the chasm which ego-mind cannot cross, your belief will need to be like hands cupped to receive fresh insight rather than clenched tightly around old certainties. You will need to offer up your belief as an embodied substance, as an expression of your being. It will need to have been formed in the crucible of your most intimate experience and tested in everyday mundane reality. Your next level of transformation, what we are calling the embrace, requires that you receive what can only be described *as a new order of being.* One in which the fragments are fused into a state of oneness and united in profound integrity. As it happens, this is a state the mystics agree, where your experience of Reality is profoundly transformed, even though you must still, *'chop wood and carry water.'*

There is a story told of the dried pebble hard chickpea taken from the sack and dropped in cool water:

"How nice," it says, "I was feeling so tight and dry, this cool water is helping me loosen up a bit." Then as the water in the pot begins to warm, the chickpea says, "Now this is utterly fantastic. How long have I waited to open up like this. This is my kind of spa. I am in ecstasy." But then as the water begins to boil the chickpea cries and screams, "Hold on, I didn't ask for this much heat. I'm being boiled alive. My God, why have you abandoned me?"

"Ah, but now," says God, "you are truly ready to offer yourself to the great Feast of Life."

For some the increments of their transformation are a steady and slow burn, for others it's as if the heat gets turned up very quickly. One thing is sure—keep transforming negative stress and remain steadfast in your commitment to growth and one day you'll notice a quality to your own being where all your hardness and dryness has been dissolved. The story suggests that to be food for the *Feast of Life* you must willingly undergo radical transformation. You offer yourself to the heat of every stress and let it take you to a place where your true nature is fulfilled. All this is about the movement from separate self to full integration with higher purpose, and in case it has not already become clear, that is not a linear trajectory. You must be so radically open that all that you have lived and believed can be transformed. Now that you have mastered the raw energy of stress and used it to carry you higher, you meet a subtler version of that energy which is going to come and blow at the very foundations of how you make meaning.

Learning to Embrace Paradox

You can't cross the chasm by trying and you cannot cross the chasm by not trying.

The *chasm* we are referring to is between dualism and non-dualism. In relation to our topic, it is the chasm between *coming to terms with stress and learning to transform its negative impact, learning how to cultivate positive energy, deciding to commit to your own growth and to discover the true value of living in integrity with an evolving moral conscience, and with emotional and psychological maturity* and *fully embracing stress as your greatest teacher without ever flinching from the truth that you can always be grateful and take the energy of every exacting test and free it, so that it helps lead you to complete unity with your Highest Self, where your most creative work flows back into the world as a reflection of that essence.*

Let's make sure that we have a clear understanding about these two rather heady terms, dual and non-dual: for those of us who are not philosophers, what do these two terms mean for us in practice?

First and foremost, we are talking about the difference between the place where we are pulled and bounced between *the charge* of opposing demands, and the place where that charge no longer has the power to send us into a tailspin. In fact, the absence of that charge takes you to a whole new territory of being. When Rumi says, "*Out beyond right and wrong, there is a field. I'll meet you there,*" he is not suggesting a morally neutral world where right and wrong do not matter. The field he is referring to is reaching the stage of your development I am describing as being on the other side of the chasm: you clearly know the crucial dimensions of right and wrong, which still hold true, but you are now going to experience right and wrong from a much deeper psychological and spiritual perspective. To do this you will have to release self-righteous convictions.

In a dualistic framework there is a law or an imperative for things to be either one way or the other: it is not only that certain things *are* right or wrong—it is that they have to be that way for you to make discerning and ethical choices. We rely on polarities for the formation of our conscience, basic codes of human decency and the body of law by which we measure our progress towards fairness and justice on planet Earth. So dualism, in this aspect of a complex topic, is not a bad thing; it uses the framework of opposites and distinctions to create order. Civilization as we know it couldn't progress without it. We probably wouldn't even have the fun of taking sides in our favorite sports games, where there have to be winners and losers.

Now believe you me, philosophers have a whole very esoteric world they enter into on the subject of dualism where they contemplate the nature of perception and how consciousness functions in relation to sense objects and experience. They explore the intricacies of self and other, subjective and objective, mind and matter. For our purposes we do not have to work out precisely how entangled mind and matter really are, if rocks are conscious or if there is a separation between the material and spiritual realms. Our subject is stress; and precisely how we can *transcend* the kind of stress which leaves us running feverishly between a thousand forms of This or That *in order to* experience serenity of mind and the creativity of our highest self. Non-dualism is the state of mind where all the stressful charge around, 'it *has* to be *this or that*,' is dissolved and your energy no longer gets trapped in false dilemmas. The energy of stress, which is none other than raw energy, sees its way through to aligning with the core of your being. We call this spiritual mastery.

We have noted from the outset, this is not necessarily the easiest way forward but the path which becomes an expression of your true self. Remember in this state, even when you are wronged by others, you use that energy to take you higher not bring you down. You can only sustain that approach when your seat of consciousness is in the non-dual. If you get caught in the charge of persecuted and betrayed mind, you throw the energy ball back into the court where it will ricochet for as long as you play that 'game.' *In the non-dual state there is nothing to ricochet against.* There is only energy which is going to facilitate more opening, more growth, more humanizing and more illumination.

In a dualistic framework we tend to think that this energy must be either fiery or cooling; only in the non-dual state can we appreciate a fire so intense that it burns through to bring relief to the soul.

In *the embrace* you taste that burning through as your highest liberation, no longer do you live in the place of *pain is bad* and *pleasure is good.* Therefore, I must seek pleasure and avoid anything that is painful. You understand that pain, which is an expression of stress, is the messenger and you don't shoot the messenger. You are only interested in how you can learn to ride the energy to go to your highest self. Please understand that I am not glorifying pain as an end in itself or any kind of self-gorging holy martyr complex. Pain is simply there in the design of evolution. It is expressed in varying degrees and it needs to be met as an emissary of meaning and not as a fierce enemy.

This is where paradox plays a useful role. You generally cannot use polarities of meaning to escape polarities. You need some other non-polarized ingredient. Paradox takes the framework of, 'it *must* be *this or that*' and says,

'Have you considered how it might be this and that? Have you considered an entirely different lens to apprehend the truth? Can you appreciate how something which is locked into an insurmountable contradiction at one level flows into con-

133

junction at another? Can you experience the place where the heart and the intellect synchronize?'

Deep contradictions have the power to break the hold our conditioning has over us—like a Zen Koan they can force us to explore the part of ourselves we don't usually look for answers. Contradiction can exert a kind of unbearable pressure on the rational mind which pushes us into the territory of insight and intuition.

We have all had experiences where a few moments of stillness took us further than hours of scurrying around looking for an answer; or found ourselves so frustrated and perplexed by something that we gave up trying to force a solution—and when we did, lo and behold, what we needed immediately presented itself. Or when, on the surface, we achieve success and receive more than our share of accolades only to realize that we feel shallow and empty; or conversely, when so much has been taken away and we might justifiably be at a low ebb, we find a mysterious current of new life carrying us places we had hardly dared to dream of.

Paradox and contradiction help us to see that there is more at play than meets the eye. We see that there are bigger forces at work and that our propensity to want to contain reality in manageable bite sized chunks only encourages us to live inside stories that are much too small and fragmented for us.

Paradox creates a bridge between the reality we have come to expect and the reality that exists entirely outside of the box of our somewhat predictable expectations.

Let's examine the paradox: *"You can't cross the chasm by trying and you can't cross the chasm by not trying."* In attempting to unpack this or any other paradox you will see that it loses some in translation—part of its power is in allowing the mystery of the contradiction to work on you and to let it till the soil of your imagination. Paradox will not provide you with a literal truth. Attempts to make it literal only sacrifice its more expansive and suggestive dimensions. With that little advisory, let us proceed to unpack the statement above.

'*You can't cross the chasm by trying,*' is a way of encoding the knowledge that up to this point in your development you have had to rely on directing *conscious will and intention* to transform your relationship to stress, but that creates an unfortunate by-product. You think your growth has resulted from your effort alone. Not only was the *Bhagavad-Gita* written to correct you on that point, a mighty chorus of spiritual teachers through the ages confirm that this is a blunder. After all, you cannot take credit for the primary energy in the universe which came to you as your teacher, nor can you take credit for the effects and results that were associated with your learning to work cooperatively rather than antagonistically with it.

You learned to open the door when the universe came knocking—big deal! It is at this point you will discover the way forward is impossible for those who lack humility. Why? Because humility is a form of awe and reverence for the true nature of reality which gives one an *accurate* perspective on one's own role in the vastness of Life's unfolding. Humility is a form of knowledge which is gained through experience. Those who have it are decidedly less negatively stressed, for obvious reasons.

The other embedded wisdom in '*You can't cross the chasm by trying,*' comes from the idea that in order to try something you have to have a pre-set notion or conceptual basis for the idea you're going to try out—the problem there is your *concepts* come from a dualistic paradigm; they don't have the medicine to carry you to a reality which is beyond their own framework.

'*You can't cross the chasm by not trying,*' also encodes the idea that neither are you going to get anywhere by sitting back and passively expecting the universe to resolve your dilemma. '*Not trying*' suggests that you have abandoned any form of will, intention or purpose. You have learned that progress into this new territory, where entirely different rules apply, can't be gained by regular effort so you try its opposite. By making no effort you're still in the mind of 'if it is not *that*, it must be *this.*' This is a good example of what Einstein referred to when he observed, "*You cannot solve a problem at the same level of consciousness that created it.*"

You are also still holding back in the old, '*Is it going to be* up *or is it going to be* down?' mind. Behind that question is ego, not Newtonian physics. The mind is trying to calculate, '*What if I try and I don't succeed?*' By now, you have learned *that* is a self torturing, '*Will I be able to handle the stress of failure?*' question. A question which transforms negative stress is: '*What might I learn if I don't succeed? What can I gain from trying?*'

There can be no holding on if you are to cross the chasm—it is like asking the dualistic framework to provide you with a guarantee that it will save you if you take a leap. Yes, of course it will be there. If you haven't gone beyond it as a framework it will still be there to offer you comfort, like training wheels until they are shed.

As long as you remain incapable of resolving this dilemma you will not be able to experience the full embrace of stress and the liberation that comes with this more advanced stage of spiritual development. You will not be able to merge with the full creative potential of your highest self. Make no mistake about it, this advanced stage of spiritual development was once thought to be reserved for the Masters of wisdom. Its accomplishment was considered to be remote and inaccessible to the average person. But the tide has been rising, as wave upon wave of collective consciousness strengthens and intensifies. *The so-called average person* has begun to demonstrate capacities for transformation hitherto not witnessed on such a massive scale.

So let's see if we can experience the essence of the Paradox. '*You can't cross the chasm by trying and you can't cross it by not trying.*' Since this cannot be literally true and its meaning cannot be understood by hammering away at simple logic or by pressing the rational mind to cough up the answer, one must take another approach.

Some of you will remember that the poet Shelley suggested that in order to fully enter a work of art to apprehend the scale of its meaning and its beauty one would have to, "*suspend disbelief.*" We have this capacity to suspend the momentum of the conditioned mind and enter into a space where we are radically open. This openness, this ability to tell the mind that there is something new to behold also requires full permission for the imagination to engage with what is being apprehended. That exalted feeling you get when you are lifted into a piece of music or a poem or a painting happens when you experience the substance of the artist's imagination and you literally come alive to it and let it interact with the substance of your own being.

What is being described here is the active and fully engaged dimension of receptivity. It's almost as if at this level, everything carries *within* it the seeds of its opposite, not *outside* of itself. Like the *Yin-Yang* symbol which holds the seed of light within the darkness, and the seed of darkness within the light. So the '*trying*' and '*not trying*' are enfolded in each other until they merge.

How do you get to cross the chasm?

By summoning up your most passionate and engaged receptivity to be fully present to what is given; by holding open a space for your deepest intuition to enter into you to prompt creative action; and when you act, knowing the difference between inspiration and grandiosity; audacity and bravado, conviction and persuasion. By probing the Mystery, and then surrendering inside it, you let the embrace become mutual and simultaneous: giving everything you have to the universe, and receiving from it all that you are capable of receiving. If that sounds like a form of making love, you are on the right track.

You are probably familiar with mystics talking about the state of oneness accessed though encounter with the Mystery, but an astronaut? Edgar Mitchell was the sixth man to walk on the moon. As he was returning to planet Earth there in his spinning capsule, he had an experience which the Hindus refer to as *Nirvakalpa Samadhi*: complete immersion in the state of oneness. *Edgar shifted from observing the universe to an entirely different state of being in which the universe was flowing through him.* He was no longer separate. His consciousness had crossed the chasm on one side of which he and the universe were separate and on the other side they were one. When he headed to the moon his consciousness was in a dualistic framework but not when he was headed home. Now that's creative stress!

Once you reach the other side of the chasm, it is not as if you are now permanently on vacation, or singing to the bluebird on your shoulder. There is still a climb ahead, but things are decidedly different as you embrace the very issues you ran from and which caused you so much trouble.

9

Entering the Highest States of True Equanimity

When you are trying to acquire a new skill one of the first things you calculate is the relative ease or difficulty involved. If the skill in question is easy and you progress fast you generally continue until you've reached the desired level of mastery. If acquiring the skill is difficult you'll need more motivation, and if it's really hard you will need to muster considerable tenacity if you are not to give up. Overcoming difficulties, particularly great ones, can bring a sense of triumph and satisfaction and that precious sense of reward which comes from hard effort. Whether your accomplishment is easy or difficult, in the long run what counts is how much satisfaction you gain from the particular skill you have acquired and how important mastering this skill is in the overall story of your life.

Mastering stress is similar. You must learn the skill of *encountering* energy when it comes to you—not deflecting it into angst, self-pity, irritability or blame, but channeling its raw power to fuel your higher creativity, emotional, psychological and spiritual development. In this case, once you begin to advance, you see that the shift in skill levels brings with it a shift in meaning. You see that stress, if negatively charged, obstructs many things in your life and leaves you exhausted, but if positively engaged, opens a door to more fulfillment, more meaning and more purpose in your life.

When we look at anything through the lens of *easy or difficult* we immediately ask ourselves what is it worth to us if we are going to face difficulties—what is the pay off? What is our reward going to be? What is the most cost effective way can we make it happen? When we attempt to look through the lens of wholeness and integration our question is located *in the heart of meaning itself. As new thought metaphysics reminds us, we begin in the affirmation of wholeness and then embrace the way the universe leads us to that wholeness. You cooperate with subtle energy rather than constantly trying to force outcomes.*

As you gain mastery with stress you become more attuned to the subtle call of your inner nature which hitherto had been drowned out by the loud '*pay attention to me*' voice of unattended or unresolved stress. That subtle voice of your intuition is, believe it or not, part of your wilder nature—it doesn't always bubble up with soft and comforting ideas. Your deeper intuitions often contain more radical content. They send a message from your core that maybe you should sell your house, give up your job, move abroad, live more simply, take a pay-cut and work on a social justice issue, take on a huge responsibility, start from scratch on a new career, keep doing what you're doing even when the odds are against you, lead a community revitalization effort or go into deep seclusion for a period. They also carry psycho-spiritual content: '*despite the obvious danger, trust the moment*'; '*be doubly generous even when you are feeling pinched*'; '*let the worst unfold and be happy about it'; 'be grateful even when it would be easier to feel a scalding resentment.'*

We are not talking about impulsiveness here but how to recognize and respond to authentic inner guidance. When you have learned how to discern the difference between the two, you will be well on your way to attunement with your higher self. What I am calling the embrace of stress requires this *constant sensitive attunement to the subtle signals and energy changes around you—you catch the breeze before it becomes a tempest.*

One of the markers which confirms that you have achieved an advanced level of development is the emergence of *true equanimity* in your life. And equanimity is nothing like the dull pretense of flatland which we discussed earlier. It is a place where the world cannot buffet you from staying in the current of what you value most or from living in resonance with your own higher self. You are unwilling to sacrifice the circuitry of inner communion and well-being that comes from having achieved a degree of integrity with your own beautiful, quirky, original self. This state of equanimity is often associated with the idea of *flow* since even high velocity energies seem not to have the capacity to displace you from being centered. But equanimity does not really translate as a facile version of, *'going with the flow.'* It can as easily mean going against the flow of lower energies and conditioned mind, but in a manner that is not disruptive to your own inner peace.

Flow, in the spiritual sense, contains the paradox of moving with, and not moving with. In this sense, *flow is about moving with the inner obedience and surrender to the truth of higher self*, whether or not that moves us into or away from the stream of activity around us. Flow, paradoxically, is that movement which is anchored in the faith that any given moment has its truth which must be faced.

Equanimity has a quality of stillness and assurance which supports this facilitation of deep flow. It is not to be confused with *'whatever'* which is a marker of negative stress: *'I don't have the energy to care about it. So, whatever,'*

—preferably intoned with a vapid air and a Brooklyn accent! Acquiescence is a way of succumbing to stress, true equanimity never compromises its passionate engagement in representing the truth of its beliefs but it does so in a way that reflects advanced emotional and psychological maturity.

Imagine *now a capacity to face the truth of any given moment and never subverting it, or rejecting it, or denying it, because it isn't what you want or think you need to deal with.*

Imagine *the kind of presence that comes with such a stance and the gift of knowing that you're living in high integrity with who you are, not necessarily who the world wishes you to be.*

When viewed from this perspective, equanimity is not about being *Mr. Cool as a Cucumber* when all around you people lose their heads. It's about living in the continuous flow of knowing that whatever your next move will be, it won't be about whether it's easy or difficult, it will be about whether it is really right for you and whether it liberates you to express your unique creativity in any given situation.

Equanimity knows that reality plays with multiple variables and so it is always prepared to accept that random variables will present themselves in shaping final outcomes. Thus, it knows how to let preconceived notions dance with surprise elements. In this regard it knows that chaos plays a significant role in engendering the next level of order and that holding too tightly to order engenders the next level of chaos. Equanimity is a state of trust—not in your own perfect wisdom (*that is hubris*), but that whatever you learn in the process of acquiring wisdom will be most welcome. For you have already discovered on this path that a deep commitment to learning brings joy.

Now imagine what seems enormously difficult from one perspective: the mother who loses her son to addiction or a drug overdose; the young person whose spouse goes off to war and is killed or who returns psychologically scarred; the ballerina who is crippled in a car accident; the young intellectual who is imprisoned by an oppressive government, and all those who face what could be devastating stress—imagine them facing these challenges with deep equanimity. See them transform their own suffering in ways that remind us that so called *average people* can, and do, demonstrate strength and courage we tell ourselves belongs exclusively to our special heroes. For some, tragedy becomes an initiation which propels them to surrender to their own greatness and spiritual depth and to completely re-appraise what it means to live a meaningful life.

One of those people who taught me about equanimity—never to be confused with emotional flatness which comes from fending off excitation or depression—was a friend who was in the midst of an aggressively successful financial investment career when his son died of a drug overdose in his first year in college. He lived through the pain as his teacher and before long had radically reorganized his life to become a major force in philanthropy, eco-justice and corporate reform. He is one of those quietly luminous people you look at and wonder, 'How did he learn to live with such integrity and find his way to being so centered and balanced?'

So, on your own journey to these high states, however mundane your initiations and learning process, look into the eyes of one of those *"quietly luminous"* average people and ask them their story. *Your spiritual teachers are all around you*!

Equanimity Part Two: Authentic Passion

Our reportage of stress in our lives often takes the form of *drama* and more than we would like to think—*melodrama*. It generally requires a sympathetic ear from others, but unless it is of a more compelling or tragic nature, it generally gets a private yawn. After all, we tell ourselves it is a practically unavoidable modern day disease which we all share. *'Tell me about it! I had 500 hundred e-mails in my in-tray to respond to!'*

When stress moves beyond the 21*st* Century versions of *'woe is me'* to being boldly engaged and embraced, it emerges as the energy of authentic passion: your body and mind, as well as your heart and soul, synchronize in an optimal way to release their creative energy. This kind of refined passion is in sharp contrast to undisciplined emotionality and the kind of ungrounded intensity which passes for passion and which is only commendable in one's adolescent development. Genuine passion arises out of the cauldron of testing and commitment, the gestating power of vision and the fecundity of imagination.

You know when you are in the presence of this kind of passion, it is energizing. It searches out those places in you where your own deeper frequencies desire to be met. In the presence of great passion you can feel exalted. You feel invited to participate, whether it is at the level of ideas, emotions or actions; or you feel sincerely challenged and even quickened by the kind of passion that asks you, *'How long have had your head in the sand? Are you drugged, sleepwalking? Look at what is happening to your planet, have you really become so numbed? How did your fire grow so dim?'* Sometimes these kinds of questions are like a fresh wind blowing through your life. When you experience passion coming from the heart of your deepest awareness it will not take a polarizing form. Again, we find ourselves in the paradox that passion emerging from deep consciousness and spiritual intention expresses itself with true equanimity.

Hold a picture in your mind of someone whose passion activated and inspired your own. Try to remember someone whose passion awakened your heart's core, rather than someone who was able to stir mental fury in you.

Notice how contemplating the quality of their passion helps reveal something about the essence of this person. It allows for contact at a much deeper level. It is as if you get to witness the living substance of their heart or mind, or even the fullness of their being and something of your own essence is aroused. Whether it was an artist or scientist, a politician or an activist with whom you felt this quickening, recall that quality in their presence which reflected creative stress. See how something in their personal field tells you how faithfully they grappled with visions, ideas, obstacles in their path, the skepticism or obstruction of others, or their dedication to the muse.

Being in the presence of really deep passion is a spiritual experience and a great reminder of what is really behind evolutionary progress. Barbara Marx Hubbard reminds us that one of the greatest contributions we can make towards peaceful planetary civilization is to live into the question, '*What does my heart most truly desire?*' Follow that question all the way in and you cannot but come home to a vitality of passion which will carry you over every hurdle on the way to your higher self.

Equanimity is not achieved by trying to live a balancing act between what will be most and least stressful—what we are referring to here lies across that chasm. On one side you found yourself always battling competing priorities, as if somehow you could find the perfect accommodation in life; on the other side, you are the embodiment of that balance, you have actually entered into the state of balance, which as we have noted, is a very alive and engaged place to be. This has to be a place, if it exists in Reality, where there is contraction *and* expansion, expansion *and* contraction—not a place where the expanded perpetually rules in some kind of endless euphoria; a place where if you're not getting enough of the expanded there must be something wrong with you. But it is a place where joy is met, like the rhythm of the breath, inhaled and then exhaled. In every moment, in the rhythm of the universe and on a vast scale, suns are exploding and stars are being born; in our lives something is always being given and something is taken away; in Nature something is in one form and then it transmutes into another form; in any story ending is the prelude to beginning and loss is the precursor to discovery.

Live outside this truth and it is just pretty philosophy, live inside it and you will know what it is like to be both hospice worker to final exhalation and midwife to first breath. You will understand how the universe was designed for co-creativity so that you literally participate in bringing things to an end as much as giving birth to new life. This deep equanimity names the ending of things with fierce courage and gives passionate support to new forms. If you have ever been in its presence you will have witnessed its raw power. That is why great teachers do not have time to be nice and beat around the bushes to make sure your feelings don't get hurt. They want to draw you into the Circle of Life where contraction is the prelude to birth.

Equanimity embodies this respiration of the real! It allows for the deepest embrace of the things that present themselves as our most difficult dilemmas because it no longer seeks the preferential treatment or partisan endorsement of a divided and polarized mind. Anyone who can reach such a state on an express train please proceed, for those who prefer the hike, let us share the beauty of every boulder on the path, the magnificent sheer cliffs, the towering dark forests and the inexpressible beauty that comes when you have almost reached complete exhaustion and you turn around and look down on the incomparable vista provided by the climb.

The Very High State Of Not Forcing Anything

The road to hell is paved with very powerful people getting what they want.

Ever try really hard to get what you wanted and then recognize it really wasn't what your *heart desired*. Stress does that doesn't it? It sends you scurrying after things that you're supposed to want. It's got that energy of, *"Got to have it."* It puts your own heart's desire in the deep freeze and tricks you into believing that the really important thing is to get on board with what everybody else is dreaming about. And the thing about that collective dream is that it has a huge unconscious pull—even when it is quite subliminal, you find yourself being pulled into dreams that have been marketed to you, but which, when you examine them, do not come from your higher self at all.

So here's something to consider: the more you are pulled by this collective force field, the greater your stress will be. *Whenever you are trying to catch up with something that is not an expression of your true self, you will experience negative stress and whenever you follow your heart's desire, you will experience creative stress.*

To be able to discern the difference between your heart's desire and a very compelling fantasy is absolutely essential; it is why I have placed so much emphasis on attunement with the core self, listening to intuition and developing subtlety. Observe it closely, and you will see how your true heart's desire reveals itself while the counterfeit version will always attempt to force situations to be a certain way so that you can achieve what you want.

It takes extraordinary power to be able to avoid getting sucked in to the lower energy dimensions of the collective force field. The power of which we speak is capable of shedding intense social conditioning, ingrained family patterns, and dealing with the tsunamis of massive peer pressure and the opinion of the majority. In fact in its *apogee,* this power is capable of influencing the entire social field in ways that draw its energies upward as part of *an evolutionary vanguard of higher consciousness.*

Remember that the trapped energy of negative stress does not go away, it awaits release. A great spiritual teacher is one who can facilitate, for large numbers of people, the release of that trapped energy, so that it moves toward higher and subtler frequencies. Truth has such power that again and again throughout the history of our human species we have seen how it transmutes the energy of hatred and transforms the social order.

Now we have reached a time in our evolution *when the work of great spiritual teachers is increasingly the work of conscious people everywhere* who are demonstrating that these powers and capacities to transform the social field are becoming more widespread and gaining momentum. Great teachers are always way showers. They are profound exemplars who show us how to stand in the fires of every negative stress, condemnation, corrupt self-interest and transform those energies into love and forgiveness. Now the pathways for these creative spiritual capacities are expanding exponentially as the sheer numbers of people engaged in self-development, humanitarian work, consciousness-raising and spiritual practice increases across the planet. This expansion of consciousness comes at a time when it is desperately needed: at an alarmingly rapid rate, some of the vital functions of our planet are becoming severely compromised.

As with any crisis, there is a tendency to want to force through the quickest and easiest solutions rather than address underlying causes—anything that won't require us to collectively *face the music* that we are a species which is devastating its own habitat. What is called for is nothing less than a whole new way of being: a new social and planetary order in which a maturing humanity engages in a values revolution that re-directs our creativity towards peace, deep emotional intelligence, and postmodern lifestyles which sustain our longing for communion with each other and with the teeming life around us.

Our work now is to recreate the social field at a much higher octave of consciousness—but such an ambitious goal cannot be accomplished by forcing it to happen. And it begins with each one of us reaching closer to our own highest self and its frequencies of refined passion, equanimity and deep facilitation of growth and conscious evolution. Out of this higher consciousness we will be able to tap into creative capacities to address world problems at a level beyond egoic greed and insatiable consumption.

How do we make real progress without forcing or without trying to make things happen according to a predetermined design? We know it is certainly not by being laid back nor is it by being supremely pushy. We discover that somewhere between the negative and the false positive there is a *true positive* which gets revealed. When we discover the true positive it literally unfolds in a movement with reality that synchronizes with other aspects of what is real and true around it.

Truth is ultimately self-revealing and found not to be separate from other deep truth: so we are talking about something which gathers momentum in our consciousness and becomes alive and generative rather than being pushed or cajoled. We are not talking about an energy which feels the need to run out and convert others. It is more an energy which catches fire or which radiates out, so that others are attracted to its light. In the Embrace you become *the embodiment* of deeper truth, not its *'sales rep.'*

The great teachers eschew missionary proselytizing which tries to convince people that *their* religious beliefs are wrong and that *yours* are right. When you are in the presence of awakened consciousness and deep spirituality it will call you to it. It will reveal itself to you. *Imagine* now developing to such an extent in your own life that you become more and more of an attractor for the real and true to unfold around you wherever you go. Again we associate this level of consciousness with a high degree of spiritual mastery, but enough have accomplished this state that it is now more accessible to larger numbers of people.

But let me reinforce the notion that this liberated state does not translate as niceness and sweetness—it brings *the fire that burns up the pretend reality of the shimmer world.* It speaks truth to power. And as we know, all too well, it can attract both blame and seduction, which attempt to drag it back into the lower stress game of easy rewards or fear of losing out. *Great truth always finds itself out of sync with the dying paradigms but hugely synchronized with the worlds that are coming into being.*

When you are permanently in a state where you are a stable attractor for reality to reveal itself in your presence, you are at the level of a spiritual teacher. Synchronicities will be so numerous that people will be able to feel your shakti, or blessed energy. In fact what is unfolding at those very, very high levels of consciousness is that the basic raw energy of the universe, coming at any velocity of potential stress, *meets awareness seated in equanimity* and passes upwards into a more refined and subtle state. I have known several teachers who have achieved this capacity, and lest you think it is completely unattainable for us mere mortals, at least to some advanced degree, let me tell you about two Vietnam Vets who attained it at quite advanced levels.

Two Enlightened Vietnam Vets

The first story was told to me by a very spiritually attuned person who had been invited to Fort Bragg for a couple of days to give some lectures on the Middle East. He told me that he had been assigned to a Sergeant who met him at the airport and took him everywhere he needed to go throughout his stay. What struck him almost immediately about his escort was the quality of full attention which he gave to everything from opening a door to the back-and-forth of conversation. He had that unmistakable fullness of presence that one associates with a person who has done a lot of inner work. By the end of their time together my friend was so impressed with how conscious and tuned in this man was, that he asked him if he would be willing to share his spiritual practice. What his escort shared with him was this: in Vietnam, his work was to clear mines. It was a deeply stressful assignment; one in which he had to confront his own fears. Every moment demanded his utmost attention; he could not allow himself to be distracted. Every step he took he had to make a conscious choice. Every step he took he celebrated life. This was his practice: to give his full attention to every moment and to celebrate every step in life. When he left Vietnam he continued every step of his life in gratitude.

His practice is the essence of the Embrace. Perhaps you might want to see how many steps you can take in full awareness and deep gratitude. Tune in, and you'll find that there are more of these invisible saints walking in our midst than you ever suspected.

The second story starts with a young man growing up in rural Oklahoma. His family is a modern-day mix of Native and European ancestry. He is sent to a missionary school where native spirituality is suppressed and where he experiences some molestation. From time to time he finds himself called to the woods to rekindle his deeper memory of his real spiritual inheritance. He knows that the deeper teachings of Christianity can be integrated with authentic ancient teachings which do not separate humans from all other life in nature.

His name is Sequoyah. He is very bright, physically agile, with advanced linguistic and communication skills. He is recruited into Army intelligence, learning several Asian languages. His role in Vietnam and surrounding areas is military Intel work, which involves being dropped into remote areas and surviving in extremely hostile and adverse conditions. During this period he is given drugs to increase his stamina and help him stay awake for days on end. Not unlike a number of other Vietnam Vets, he left Vietnam with a drug problem. It was a problem which was to lead him to a harsh prison sentence at Leavenworth penitentiary.

Yet it was here in prison that he was finally able to reach deep enough into his own being to make contact with his core self—his higher self. Prison time became a golden opportunity to focus on his spiritual development, spending time in meditation, doing yoga and exploring the capacities of his own consciousness. It became clear to the authorities that not only was he a model prisoner, he was a luminous being. And through the right interventions and great good fortune, he was released.

Sequoyah is an advanced spiritual teacher who shares his wisdom, which is an integration of the perennial philosophy and native ways. In his presence you learn what it is to be fully surrendered to the grace of the moment; to have no fixed ideas about how things should or ought to be; and to forgo being judgmental. He shares a prayer which came to him while living with the remarkable Kogi people on a mountain in Colombia. This is a summation of his prayer: Great Thanks, Great Peace, Great Love.

Practice: Great Thanks, Great Peace, Great Love

Breathe in great thanks until you are filled with gratitude. Breathe out great thanks offering thanks to everything in creation. This gratitude allows for peace to arise.

Breathe in great peace until you are filled with peace. Breathe out great peace to resonate with everything in creation. This peace allows for love to arise.

Breathe in great love until you are filled with love. Breathe out great love to everything in creation. This love allows for endless gratitude to arise.

To be in the presence of someone who is not trying to squeeze reality into the time frames, purposes and needs which *they* have, but who is completely comfortable with things as they *unfold*, is to be in the presence of the miraculous nature of reality as it is. Trusting in this unfolding process requires the dissolution of controlling and defensive habits and rather than being an attitude of 'anything goes' it is one in which deep awareness makes contact with, and gives full permission to what is trying to arise.

To live in this state is to live a guided life. You are now someone who is consciously cooperating with your own Higher Self. Even when you sense that a scorching wind is what is arising, you cooperate with it and know you will bend as it blows. You are now flexible and transparent. You are able to move with life's expansions and contractions and not blocked by your own hidden agendas which gauge their response on the basis of concealed fine print which lays out the tightly proscribed conditions under which you will be transparent and flexible.

As it turns out, those conditions etched in fine print, begin to reveal themselves when you have cleared out a lot of the negative stress in your life. You're freer than you have ever been, your life is nourished and you've learned how to sustain the nourishment. You know what pulls you out of alignment and how to restore a profound sense of equanimity. You feel the presence of your higher self pulling you inexorably towards the summit of your journey. You feel the silver capped crystalline snows of your personal Everest. But out of the corner of your eye you see dark purple-grey storm clouds forming. What do you suppose this '*last barrier*' will be?

You have come such a long way; I suggest you read the fine print—that is where the shadow waits and hides. But this time, given all the work you have done, grace is on your side. And ready to intervene at precisely the right moment.

10

Embracing Grace and Releasing All Conditions

Grace and the Shadow

Negative stress does not need to be glaringly obvious. It slips in as you route whatever energy comes at you through filters which unknowingly or unconsciously create a distorted picture of reality. Perhaps only an Avatar is without any kind of distorting filters. Until we are in such an enlightened state where any energy that comes towards us, no matter what its velocity or intensity, is internally drawn upwards by higher consciousness, we will have to keep working to see how these filters function and how, even at very subtle levels, they polarize energy.

Filters help us make an instantaneous judgment about any energy in the field around us. They can operate quite effectively as a hidden code buried in the subconscious. But the code tends to be binary---either positive or negative. This binary code is embedded in the template of your personal narrative: win-lose, success-failure, good-bad, right-wrong, punishment-reward, admired-rejected etc. It is equally embedded in our collective narrative: in-group-out-group, good guys-bad guys, rich people-poor people. And as noted earlier this binary code plays a role in our moral development and in creating order in society. But you get to a point in your development where you recognize that there is much more to reality than the binary code.

Maturity at all levels, from individual to societal, requires that we advance to a more complex, nuanced and integrated psychological development. We move *from either-or*, which we know in its extreme forms has very lethal consequences, *to both-and* with its more subtle dance of inclusions which allows for your truth and my truth to coexist. The *either-or* that we are referring to is represented by a form of consciousness which is *threatened* by including other ideas, beliefs and ways of being. It has a large archive of filters built around *us* and *them*.

We have explored how paradox can help us transcend duality and embrace a more holistic, interdependent and interconnected framework. But *in the end we have to contemplate the nature of the shadow which is the by-product of simple binary codes such as good versus evil.* Up until this moment you probably have not been aware that the trajectory of your emotional, psychological and spiritual liberation from the coils of corrosive negative stress actually *has its own shadow side* and that you must face that shadow material if you are to progress further.

Yes, stress and the shadow are intimately acquainted. You will recall in the earliest stages of your development that the central issue you had to tackle was stress avoidance and, in many ways, the approach that got you through, in some form or other, was learning to live in integrity with your core self; and by so doing find higher ground and more personal peace of mind. But invariably you have been rejecting one thing to affirm another. Your shadow world of embedded filters is much more sophisticated than meets the eye. But the threshold that you are now about to cross requires that you embrace the whole story, not just the good parts. Especially significant are the parts those unconscious filters attempt to discard.

Meeting the shadow precipitates another helpful crisis in your development. The Embrace represents a discontinuous leap in your development. To reach your highest self you have to let go of anything which would hold you back where you feel safe living in *judgment* of self and others—the places where the shadow actually presents itself *as* your higher self. To grow, in the exponential way now called for, any traces of the artificial self have to be dissolved, leaving you completely in touch with, and reliant upon, the true self.

To dive into the core self you must have the abandonment of a caterpillar, whose screens and filters pull it back to the comfort of solid earth and a reliable food supply, yet it dissolves limited code in favor of its journey into air, light and a world of fragrance.

To keep it interesting, the final approaches to deep integration with your highest self should contain some *surprise element*, some final challenge. After all, to find yourself living in the presence of your own highest consciousness, to be alive and fully integrated into your soul's work is such an inexpressible achievement for anyone, that the final threshold to such a state must be impenetrable to anything but the total embrace of wholeness and the unified and synchronized frequencies of body, heart, mind and spirit.

When you are truly ready to embrace the shadow, you will be joined and supported, invisibly at first, *by a mysterious grace*.

Look back and you will see how instrumental the shadow has been in pointing you and nudging you towards the territory of positive values and virtues which you have cultivated on the journey. But even more importantly, the shadow also contained its own aspect of virtue. The shadow has its own seed of light.

Let's explore this challenging idea of grace and the shadow through a specific lens:

At first you discovered that you were, say, an angry person and that your response to stress was to vent anger or bottle it up inside you. Then you learned how to face those deeper issues and frustrations in your life which were making you angry. You learned how to transform this negative and damaging anger into more constructive and positive ways of communicating. You experienced the reward of taking what was a negative pattern and transforming it into creative action. But if you are like many of us you became averse to that original energy, so you learned how to keep it at bay. This is what I call *false equanimity*—the equanimity you have developed is dependent upon, in this example, a subtle avoidance of raw anger. It is a form of "*Once bitten, twice shy.*" Nonetheless, you make progress.

You also dealt with the stress-anger syndrome by cultivating the witness so that you could literally experience the quality of your energy as perceived by your higher consciousness but not get hooked by it and not re-activate it. It seemed as if everything was dealt with. Yet now you discover that there is still residual judgment, submerged fear or maybe even a little superiority. Look closely enough and you have made anger wrong. In order for you to be right, it had to have been wrong. And so you sent the ugly side of anger—the part that hurt you or hurt other people—into the shadows.

What we are talking about here is subtle avoidance. You have put in place subtle conditions and exceptions to make sure that your anger will not return in the form in which you become its victim or its instigator. At this level, the subtle filter becomes very significant and if not dealt with it can you set you back. It can become the Sisyphus trigger which rolls your rock back down the mountain.

We have all experienced these maddening regressions and deep perplexity about how we get stuck in the same old stuff. It can feel as if there are certain kinds of negative stress which we will never be able to overcome. *That is when grace enters into the picture*—completely mysterious in its own timing, it enters the story in response to your sincerity and tenacity.

Finally it comes to meet you—the storm which gathers on your otherwise perfect horizon. You were able to skillfully transmute a dysfunctional response to anger and you thought it was over, but there in the fine print you now see it was conditional on it never being '*THAT*.' You may find yourself skewered because precisely THAT is what has showed up. Funny, when we set conditions and try to impose them on reality, *'I can handle anything but That,'* guess what chooses its exquisitely awkward moment to show up?

'What is THAT for you? How can it be embraced?'

It is usually a form of energy that you find ugly in yourself and it seems to be a thread in your storyline—part of you that is jealous, greedy, lascivious, proud, vain and so forth. It takes the form of incidents, breakups, confessions, vows to reform or something you are always trying to keep the lid on. When you think it has gone from the story it has an uncanny ability of showing up in another form, as if it will never go away. It is one of the portals for negative stress: when the raw energy of the universe comes towards you in that particular form, you distort it in the same place over and over again. Despite the fact that you find everything else clearing and that you are so ready to give your full self to an impassioned, healthy and creative life, there is one place where love seems not to penetrate. One place left where there is the energy of fear, loathing or addictive attraction buried deep below the surface.

Then one day, if you are ready for the Embrace, *grace pulls you into the heart of the shadow* and you see what it is carrying. There it is, that raw, elemental fire that you couldn't handle; the fire you touched before you were ready and it burned. And it burned ugly.

But in the presence of grace—*the high witness of the whole story*—you see the gift which the shadow holds. This is what that moment is like:

There it is, erupting out of nowhere: the storm cloud, boiling with perceived malevolence. This time there is no way to run from it and it is going to cover you with its fury. But in a moment of grace, you open to it—you just abandon yourself to the storm and it lashes around you; rather than fear or loathing you feel a burst of exhilaration, as energy which was deeply trapped, rushes to the surface and is released. You love its intensity. 'No more dribbles,' you say to yourself. 'If it's going to pour, let it pour!'

Have you ever been in such a storm?

Have you ever stood in the fire of someone's anger and found yourself opened up and even deeply cleansed by it? Instead of being burnt by it, it was exactly the medicine you needed. What is going on here? It is a version of *when the student is ready, the master will appear.* In this case, the level we call the Embrace is when you are ready to experience a significant degree of personal mastery on the journey. It is the mastery of the integrated human being. It can even be experienced as ecstatic oneness. You are now coming home to your higher self. Believe me, this can feel as if you are literally being embraced by the universe, wave upon wave, throughout your entire being.

What is going on?

Your power has equalized—the shadow always arises where there is a power imbalance. It is a reflection of the lesson which could not be learned at the time, but there concealed in its guilt or trauma is the antidote to the toxins which have been stored—sometimes for a very long time. When your inner life begins to reach the kind of equanimity we have been talking about, distortions of power will start to look for ways to find equilibrium.

The power that was robbed from you prematurely; the power that was grabbed before you were ready for it; the power that was used to dominate, exploit or manipulate you; the power you longed for; the higher power you couldn't express—they all kept you in a state of disequilibrium.

The storm we speak of is finally welcome because you are ready for its power. You can handle it! When you experience this re-balancing, you are more and more aligned with, and seated in, your core self. The *natural power of the core* is trust, confidence and love. No wonder you are now able to dance with the very energy that used to stress you out. Finally, you are ready to jettison the very conditions that you thought were holding you together. You are finally completely ready to explore the highest unconditional states.

Unconditional Gratefulness

Okay, you can be grateful for the good and learn to accept the unwelcome, but be grateful for it all?

Gratefulness is a state of being, it is not an attitude you have to adopt, like trying to be virtuous or continuously reminding yourself that you need to be grateful. Gratefulness is not a duty or a responsibility, it is a marker of a certain degree of internal progress, something more like the result of fermentation. Of course, at some point, it did take a willful intention to crush the grapes, but thereafter your skill was to make sure the environment was optimal for the best fermentation process to happen. This is the mystery of the Embrace, it is about *allowing*, and *getting out of the way*, and *removing limiting conditions*, so that nothing can separate you from the most intimate experience of your core self.

As you achieve this, you amplify conscious awareness, which is sometimes referenced as being more present or having more presence. You have no problem engaging with whatever arises; you are not particularly focused on how successful you are handling things such as *perfect outcomes,* so much as observant of the *qualities* that different situations provoke in you.

You begin to notice your own signature blend of qualities and, when they are expressed you get tremendous relief from being authentically you. So you see how gratefulness arises out of the ground of your own being when it is fully permitted to express from essence and when it is not displaced by worry and negative stress, or disconnected from its own true nature. This sense of relief is the state of inner peace which emerges from sustained contact with and attunement to the reality of your essential qualities—what in Zen might be referred to as your *original state.*

So, gratefulness arises, it ferments and matures. It brings abundance to itself. Don't try to be grateful so much as give yourself permission to be grateful. You can go around thanking people if you like but this is something different.

When viewed from this perspective you can see why, in its essence, gratefulness is unconditional: it is a state of freedom to be. If you are frustrated and feel obstructed or unable to access or give expression to your own deepest qualities, you cannot help but feel an absence of gratefulness because your own essential creativity is blocked. You cannot be grateful for not being you, that would be nihilism. And pretending to be grateful for a life in which you are not being you is to feed yourself a daily poison. The concept of creative stress is all about recognizing that you must not swallow such a poison, and that the universe is not that cruel. It wants you to be you. It wants nothing more than your qualities to manifest and be expressed. Knowing that, it is worth greeting the fires of initiation without setting limits and conditions so that you can emerge free to be who you were born to be. In the end, there isn't a thing on that journey of liberation that you can be ungrateful for.

Unconditional Forgiveness

This one is not so easy. In fact, it is a complex topic to navigate.

We are still learning much about forgiveness at the individual level and collectively. Ultimately, from the grand panorama of an evolutionary perspective, it is not so hard to forgive our ancestors—after all we are the product of their learning, however clumsy or brutal. However, the closer it gets, the harder it is. Yet forgiveness, as an expression of our ability to bury the hatchet, make amends, move forward, re-establish harmony, release hurt, heal our deepest wounds and cease torturing judgment of ourselves and others, may be the single most important driver of our progress as a species.

And please let's not pretend this is just a matter of letting go. What we're talking about here is the essence of creative stress: the energy that we release is hardly so that we can dance a jig, but much more that we can rebuild our lives and relationships with greater awareness and compassion. Forgiveness is an expression of our awareness that we have been initiated into a greater commitment to realize our fullness and wholeness and the understanding that without forgiveness we remain a fragment of the true self. Forgiveness is an expression of commitment to *celebrate* Life.

I visualize the dancing Krishna playing his flute; calling all human souls to experience their highest resonance; tuning in to the frequencies of cosmic reality. This is the essence of Krishna whose music pierces the soul and calls it home. The word Krishna means deep dark blue; and you will see when he is represented in the physical form that his body is blue. It is said that he is blue because he has swallowed the dark poison of the world—which is nothing less than toxic resentment and spiraling animosity. He drinks down the screaming cacophony of hatred and disdain and turns them into resonant chords and rich symphonic variances of healing. As you explore the nature of forgiveness, meditate on this image of Krishna. The great mystery is that you can swallow the poison of resentment and turn it into love and compassion.

For some people the idea of unconditional forgiveness really doesn't make sense. 'How can you forgive someone if they haven't asked for forgiveness or shown contrition? For some, forgiveness is a response—a deeply generous response to a transgression. In dialogue with Fr. Michael Lapsley, a prominent pastor in South Africa close to the ANC, who had his hands blown off by a letter bomb, this is the position he took. Michael Lapsley has created *The Institute for the Healing of Memories* and is one of those profoundly luminous people I referred to in an earlier chapter. He does not believe that one can forgive in any kind of abstract way. In his own case, he would like to meet the perpetrators of the crime against him and to respond to them frankly and spontaneously should they seek his forgiveness. There is no desire for vengeance in his heart, quite the contrary, he radiates love and compassion.

Others see forgiveness as more proactive; it is something, when you are ready, that you can offer to others. Essentially this position is one in which forgiveness has to be enacted, one way or the other, because the state of un-forgiveness is self-damaging—one in which anger and resentment eat away at your own peace of mind. Professor Worthington is someone I've also had the good fortune to meet: he studied and wrote about forgiveness, and then his own mother was brutally murdered. He found that eventually he had to release any form of hatred towards the man responsible for this terrible crime. He lived through the cauldron of testing all the way from theory to the ultimate praxis.

To live with thoughts and feelings of revenge and hatred towards others is to condemn oneself to live with powerfully destructive forms of negative stress.

We know that if you are holding onto a cluster of unforgiving thoughts and feelings, you will experience cardiovascular constriction every time you recall the negative events surrounding them. Conjuring scenarios in your head where you act out ways to punish others becomes a form of self-abuse. So we know that for your own sake you have to release the negative charge surrounding people and events connected to your wounding.

In fact, you have to release the charge without any preconditions—since it is the negative charge itself which is destroying your health and peace of mind. This does not mean that you have to condone what has happened or compromise the truth. But you must make the ultimate commitment to your own healing and that means giving up any illusion that harm or injury to others will make you feel more whole. And since you are now advanced in transforming negative stress as a path to your highest self, you understand very clearly that your own core being transcends any degree of victimization.

Once that negative charge is released—unconditionally—you open up the field of possibilities. It could mean that you move on in your life irrespective of what happens to the other party, or it could mean that reconciliation and shared healing can now occur. You do not have to know—that is how creative stress works, once you transform the negative you open yourself to what next unfolds without having a preconceived notion of what that should be.

When you master that capacity you experience how synchronicity comes alive in an open field of possibilities. When energy is released in this fashion it seeks connection and resonance with other positive energies and you realize that the engine of your life-force can burn on all cylinders. The energy of unresolved conflict, resentment, wounding, or betrayal can remain stored for years. It must be freed. Once it is, rest assured that energy will soar. Often that means you will now have more energy to engage with the larger world. You will have more creative energy for family, community, service, social justice, or many of the causes which need urgent attention. You become one of those people who are not so absorbed in their own stuff that they have no energy to tackle the really important challenges that we face collectively.

Imagine that you are free to embrace your own highest purpose and you will see that forgiving yourself and others is key.

The dynamics of social healing and recovery from brutal oppression, exploitation, war and genocide are more complex. The collective charge of those wounded and exploited by depraved levels of injustice can only be transformed into creative energy for the future when the structures of oppression are dismantled, the truth is fully exposed and when a new social contract addresses the deep root causes of violence, greed, and the many faces of intolerance. There can be "*no future*" without forgiveness, Archbishop Tutu tells us. South Africa was a clear and bold experiment in this regard but it seems that there is still much to be learned about how to enact forgiveness on a grand scale to address contemporary violations and the great historical wounds of slavery, colonialism, racism and on and on. Instead of creating departments and ministries of peace to explore these issues—a real international movement is behind this idea by the way—the governments of the world invest in how best to prepare for war and subsidize the ever robust weapons industry.

This I can tell you, in my own international work, I have seen forgiveness transform the course of history. I have seen how it pulls us away from the brink of the inevitability of perpetual enmity and rekindles our humanity like no other force I have ever witnessed. Those who've been through the cauldron of the most intense and nihilistic hatred and yet come out the other side of Holocaust, genocide, or inter-communal conflict, to offer each other the embrace of deep reconciliation and human understanding, these are the ones on whose shoulders we stand. They transform the ultimate negatives and open the way for future generations to create pathways to peace. They incarnate love by looking into the jaws of hell and staring down hatred, and by taking on the work, the ceaseless, and never ending work of peacemakers.

Unconditional Love

It has all been said on the subject of love. Yet it is often the area where we find the fine print of our love contracts are loaded down with the most pernicious and impossible conditions: *The child who is loved on the condition that he/ she will somehow perfect their parents' dreams. The spouse who is loved on the condition that he fill the empty spaces in his partner's life. The friend who is loved on the condition that they never bring up those things in the past you don't want to look at.*

What is your own experience of discovering hidden conditions that eventually surfaced in an important love relationship? How about the ones you discovered were your own— conditions you may have been largely unconscious about until someone crossed your invisible trip wire?

These conditions create some of our most intense experiences of negative stress: they can create double bind, no-win situations. They lead into guilt and betrayal. They compound our stress like nothing else and they force us into numbing denial and secret lives. They can lead us into deep existential crises or cynicism and despair. In such moments we ask ourselves, *'Is all love some aspect of control, projection or the vehicle for a thousand surrogate needs to be met?' 'Is it the force which blinds us from seeing the stark truth?' 'Is it something that you have to keep working at to keep it alive?'* How can love possibly fulfill all the safety, comfort, inspiration, recognition and completion needs we place upon it?

Beyond the hype, we ask ourselves, *'Am I capable of selfless love? Do I deserve this love? Am I lovable?'* And we ask a lot of questions about the quantity and degree of love: *'Does he love me enough? Am I giving more love than I'm getting back? Does she love me as much as she loves the others? Should I commit to this love before I have more proof that it is equally shared? How much does my love for family members obligate me to take care of their needs? Why is it I feel that I can never do enough for the people I love'?*

In the light of all these questions, conditions, concerns, love would seem to be implicated in some of our greatest stress. While we stress a great deal over such things as our appearance, our reputation, our sexual appeal and money, the most profound stress comes from feeling unloved or incapable of giving love. Love needs are the source of our most intimate angst.

So it is appropriate, *as we approach the highest reaches of our emotional, psychological and spiritual development* that the universe would examine our hearts and souls to see if we were holding back and quietly concealing a cookie jar full of conditions in relation to love. *The full Embrace cannot be experienced until you have been picked clean of every caveat and condition which you place upon love.* Because you know by now that when the universe does not conform to the fine print of your conditions we have the recipe for negative stress. The Embrace is not possible where it meets the entropic pull of this kind of conditional energy.

The interesting thing about our spiritual development is that we are always pulled back to the most primary and elemental issues. While we have used the analogy of reaching the mountain top, the image of the wave, with its peaks and troughs, is more accurate. What we want to catch is that sense of rolling energy in movement, rising and falling, in a continuous expression of what is unfolding. Each wave reflects a new beginning, a new synthesis in our lives. No matter how far we rise, we must dip back into original source; we must refresh out of the whole. If we think of this as a commitment to transformation and renewal as our lifelong journey to keep lifting up liberated creative energy and then surrendering it so that it can fall back and rise once more out of wholeness—if we can feel comfortable with this idea, and each time we dive back into the wholeness of our heart, mind and spirit we see that there are energies to liberate—in the form of our issues, our work, our soul's purpose—we will be living the purest commitment to manifest our highest self.

This is the path from angst to ecstasy, returning cycle after cycle, wave after wave, without resistance to clear out more, release more, so that the current of love flows through you unobstructed and finally liberated into its own highest frequencies of communion with Life.

You do not have to invent love. As in Seqouyah's prayer, love arises naturally out of gratefulness and deep peace. But because it is surrounded by complicated tensions such as fear of rejection and is freighted with needs for recognition and affirmation, our relationship to love can get quite contorted. We find ourselves trying to *make it* happen, or frantically trying to upgrade it from a weak force to a strong one.

Often the energies we employ to turn on the spigot of love or keep it flowing are precisely the energies which block it. Frustration does not turn to love, it siphons off your energy into catchments of negative stress. In the place where you think the Embrace would be easiest, it is the hardest. Why? Because it is the true value and the gold standard of the universe. And because it is so precious, it is buried inside an enigma, which goes like this: *love is pure gold and is always free to those who have freed themselves to receive it.*

It is my deepest hope that you are freeing yourself to receive it. They say in some of the traditions that this work of freeing yourself is like polishing, scouring, removing blemishes so that your inner world shines like a spotless mirror or a pristine chalice. We know that this work is not about fixating on the negative, but on allowing yourself to be drawn upward by the pull of love until you are ready to fill with, and drink in, its absolutely free, unconditional and bittersweet nature. When you are wild and free in its presence you have reached your highest self.

Your highest self is unadorned. It is a light and a fire; it is the frequency of love and liberated consciousness so saturated in the intensity of witnessing the possibility of your total freedom that you are finally drawn home to it. Every fear that you drop, every worry, every reservation, every limitation and condition that you place upon your own wholeness of being which you choose to dissolve, will become the creative energy of your highest self entering into time and space—entering into your home, your workplace, your circle of friends, into the glowing furnace of your own heart and out into a world aching for such evolved human souls to arrive in their millions.

.index.

Index

C

D

E

F

G

M

N

O

Y

Z

Zen

Select Bibliography

A Common Humanity: *Thinking About Love and Truth and Justice*
Raimond Gita, (Routledge, 2000)

Authentic Happiness: *Using The New Positive Psychology to Realize Your Potential for Lasting Fulfillment*
Martin Seligman, (Free Press, 2004)

Consciousness and Healing: *Integral Approaches to Mind-Body Medicine*
M. Schlitz, T. Amorok, and M. Micozzi, (Elsevier, 2005)

Contemplative Science: *Where Buddhism and Neuroscience -Converge*
B. Allan Wallace, (Columbia University Press, 2007)

Conscious Evolution: *Awakening Our Social Potential*
Barbara Marx Hubbard, (New World Library, 1998)

Emergence: *The Shift from Ego to Essence*
Barbara Marx Hubbard, (Hampton Roads Publishing, 2001)

Embracing Mind: *The Common Ground of Science and Spirituality*
Allan Wallace and Brian Hodel, (Shambhala Publications, 2008)

Emotional Intelligence
> Daniel Goleman, (Bantam, 1995)

Science and the Reenchantment of the Cosmos: *The Rise of the Integral Vision of Reality*
> Ervin Laszlo, (Inner Traditions, 2006)

Social Intelligence: *The New Science of Human Relationships*
> Daniel Goleman, (Random House, 2007)

Spontaneous Evolution: *Our Positive Future*
> Bruce H. Lipton and Steve Bhaerman, (Hay House, 2009)

The Biology of Belief: *Unleashing The Power of Consciousness, Matter and Miracles*
> Bruce Lipton, Ph.D, (Mountain of Love/Elite Books, 2005)

The Great Turning: *From Empire to Earth Charter*
> David C. Korten, (Kumarian Press and Berrett Koehler Publishers, 2006)

The Living Universe: *Where Are We? Who Are We? Where Are We Going?*
> Duanc Elgin, (Berrett-Koehler, 2009)

The Possible Human
> Jean Houston, (Jeremy P. Tarcher/Putnam 1982)

The Untethered Soul: *The Journey Beyond Yourself*
> Michael A. Singer, (New Harbinger/ Noetic Books, 2007)

About The Author

James is currently Co-Director of The Social Healing Project funded by the Kalliopeia Foundation. This work has led him to Rwanda, Israel/Palestine, N.Ireland and elsewhere. He is a member of the extended faculty of The Institute of Noetic Sciences and its immediate past President. He was Executive Director of The Seva Foundation, an international health and development organization and, for ten years, was the Washington Office Director of Amnesty International. The Social Healing Project, assessing the convergence of societal healing initiatives around the world, is also collaborating with Intersections International in New York to convene frontier multidisciplinary dialogues on this theme. He is a member of the Evolutionary Leaders group founded by Deepak Chopra and Diane Williams and lectures widely on emerging worldviews, and integral approaches to social transformation. In 2010 he will be the keynote speaker at several conferences exploring the interface of science, consciousness, and societal healing. He is committed to dialogue as a practice and is engaged in dialogues at SEED Graduate Institute between native elders, physicists, and thought leaders; between Israeli and Palestinian psychologists and social workers, and contributes to dialogue on systems thinking and government policy making with the DC based Global Systems Initiatives. He has been a part of dialogue initiated with the Obama Administration on systems work and policy making. He and Dr Judith Thompson co-led a series of international dialogues called Compassion and Social Healing. His book *Creative Stress: A Path For Evolving Souls Living Through Personal and Planetary Upheaval* (April 2010) is highly praised and featured in Kosmos Journal, Spirituality and Health magazine, The Well Being Journal and dozens of other media outlets. James is also a member of the Board of Directors of The Temple of the Universe in Florida. He has numerous published essays. His latest essay, *Creative Atonement in a Time of Peril* will be published with other leading authors and practitioners by Josey-Bass later this year.

Credits &
Contact Information

Cover Image: "Cosmic Eye" by Philomena O'Dea
www.organic-mandalas.com

Organic Cosmic Mandalas by Philomena O'Dea is a photographic print series featuring extreme close-ups of dandelions. From such a vantage point, O'Dea explains, they morph into images that resemble mandalas. A Sanskrit word, "mandala" loosely translated means circle. This familiar design is a geometric/circular pattern that symbolizes the universe, among other things.

O'Dea is perhaps best known in Pittsburgh, PA for her documentation of the local peace movement. She is also drawn to nature photography, she says, "for its capacity to slow the senses as well as to fill them." Besides studying at the University of Pittsburgh and at Johns Hopkins University, she has studied, worked and lived around the world, including time in the Sudan, on the Thai-Cambodian border, in the Peruvian Amazon, and in England, India, Nepal and Kenya.

Editorial Support: Mali Rowan

www.malirowanpresents.com

Mali Rowan is Director of Mali Rowan Presents, whose mission is to produce unique events that ignite community, truth, and inherent brilliance and that also simultaneously raise awareness and support for cutting edge nonprofits exemplifying sustainable and conscious practices. For more information and event production possibilities please contact her at *mali@malirowanpresents.com*

Ms. Leach also co-founded **Living in the Fire of Change: Sacred -Action & Social Transformation, A Conference and Community -Forum** with James O'Dea, to offer a unique lateral platform for communities to address and sustain ongoing dialogue and action—facilitating a deep causal awareness of the integrative aspect of transformation.

She is also James O'Dea's Publicist. For booking questions please contact her at above email. James offers an extraordinary range of workshops and talk themes.

You can visit James O'Dea on the web at:

www.jamesodea.com